AMUSEMENTS OF SOLITUDE

Amusements of Solitude

Written by Alexander Herald

with Foreword and History by JL Herald

Copyright © 2024 JL Herald

All rights reserved.

This book or any portion thereof may not be reproduced or used in any manner whatsoever without the express written permission of the copyright owner, except for the use of brief quotations in a book review.

First Printed 1845, Arbroath, Scotland

Republished 2024, Australia

Cover Design © JL Herald 2024

ISBN: 978-0-6459915-8-1

Cover Image: Brechin Castle, *A Series of Picturesque Views of Seats of Noblemen and Gentlemen of Great Britain and Ireland,* 1880, Morris, Lydon, and Fawcett. Used under License

Images have been reproduced with permission by the National Library of Scotland.

FOREWORD
Written by JL Herald

It is with immense pride that I write this foreword for the republishing of Amusements of Solitude, authored by my great(x4)-grandfather: Alexander Herald. I only became aware of it recently, having undertaken some family genealogy research as part of learning about my own history before travelling to Scotland. As a published poet myself, reading his words gave me an insight into my family past, and I felt a deep connection to his poems and the thoughts expressed in them.

Alexander Herald was born in 1799 in Brechin, Scotland, the youngest of six sons to David Herald, a labourer at West Mill in Brechin and Elizabeth Caithness, of Stracathro. Alexander moved to Guthrie, in Forfarshire, where he married Elizabeth Methven and had 6 children. Alexander worked as the local grocer and post master until his death in 1863. He is buried at Guthrie Church. .Amusements of Solitude was published in 1845.

Living through the challenges of ill health, Alexander found solace and expression in his writing. His poetry, filled with vivid imagery and poignant reflections, offers a glimpse into his world—a world where the beauty of the Scottish countryside provided both inspiration and respite. As I read his verses, I imagine the quiet moments he spent crafting each line, finding peace in the rhythm of his thoughts.

The themes of nature, resilience, and the fleeting beauty of life that permeate his work are as relevant today as they were in 1845. In an age where the hustle and bustle often overshadow moments of quiet reflection, Alexander's poems remind us of the importance of pausing to appreciate the simple aspects of our existence.

Republishing "Amusements of Solitude" is not just an act of preserving family heritage but a way to share the timeless wisdom and beauty of Alexander Herald's poetry with a wider audience. It is my hope that readers will find comfort and inspiration in his words.

Alexanders poetry has been reproduced in whole, without changes to the text, font style, or layout, to preserve the intentions of Alexander in the way that this book is presented.

I have added a brief additional history of the Herald name in Scotland, and the history of Alexander, his parents, brothers, and children including the parishes of Stracathro, Brechin and Guthrie in the 1760s to the mid-1800s.

Judith

▼
David R Herald (living)
▼
Alan Russell Herald (b.1918)
▼
David Russell Herald (b.1886)
▼
David Houston Herald (b.1857)
▼
David Herald (b.1829)
▼
Alexander Herald (b.1799)

AMUSEMENTS OF SOLITUDE.

BY

ALEXANDER HERALD,
Guthrie

> "O Caledonia ! stern and wild,
> Meet nurse for a poetic child!
> Land of brown heath and shaggy wood,
> Land of the mountain and the flood,
> Land of my sires! what mortal hand
> Queer untie the filial band
> That knits me to thy rugged strand!"
>
> Scott.

ARBROATH:
STEWART GELLATLY.

DUNDEE : W. MIDDLETON . EDINBURGH : J. MENZIES .
LONDON : WHITTAKER AND CO .

MDCCCXLV.

DEDICATION.

TO JOHN GUTHRIE, ESQUIRE,

OF GUTHRIE,

𝔗𝔥𝔦𝔰 𝔙𝔬𝔩𝔲𝔪𝔢 𝔦𝔰 𝔯𝔢𝔰𝔭𝔢𝔠𝔱𝔣𝔲𝔩𝔩𝔶 𝔟𝔲𝔱 𝔥𝔲𝔪𝔟𝔩𝔶 𝔇𝔢𝔡𝔦𝔠𝔞𝔱𝔢𝔡,

BY ONE OF HIS TENANTS,

As the feeble efforts of a gratitude felt,

but unexpressed,

For kindness received from himself and family during

the many years which the author has sat

under his protection.

That he and they may be long spared together,

to enjoy the blessings of life,

And at last be rewarded with the recompence of the just,

Is the sincere wish of

His much obliged, humble, and obedient Servant,

A. HERALD.

PREFACE.

As the writer of the following pages, a few lines explanatory is due to readers.

Long inured to bodily suffering, and in a great measure shut out from the busy concerns of life, I have naturally enough sought a resource from my pen to beguile my weary hours. That comfort I have found in the composition of the following pieces.

Such was the origin of my poetry in days long past, when the hand of affliction pressed lighter than now; but my mind once imbued, the aerial society became sweet unto me, I cultivated the acquaintance farther, and felt that I belonged

PREFACE.

to the land of "the mountain and flood," where spirit of song is peculiar to peer and peasant: hence do we read of poetry issuing from its throne, and hence did we almost see a homely ploughman thrid his untaught fingers over its wild strung harp.

I have likewise to apologise unto those at least who consider them the productions of the untaught mind. Such is frankly allowed on my part; for what teaching can form the poet? But I have certainly passed through an education, and one that has called them into existence -the teaching of adversity under many years of pain.

With this explanation they are laid before the public, not from any wish for notoriety, for my mind was long averse to come forth as an author, and it is with a trembling and hesitating hand that I have been brought to write the name of poet at all. To subscribers and readers my best thanks are tendered. A perusal may amuse a leisure hour; and if not

PREFACE.

much instruction is gained, yet I have the satisfaction to think, that what light may be gained, is not one that dazzles to betray.

A. H.

Guthrie, 1845.

CONTENTS.

Verses to Guthrie Castle,
The Maid of the Valley, a Dream,
A Legend of Mull
The Bride of Lismore,
To a Friend, Dacca, India,
Adrian, to his Soul, when dying,
The Blind Man's Dog,
Lines to a Linnet,
A Fragment on Marco Bozzari, the Modern Greek Patriot,
On seeing Lord Byron's Birth in the British Peerage,
Mutual Love,
The Author's Father. - 1829,
To the Robin,
Innate Philosophy,
Recollections,
On the Snow-Drop,
Paul before Agrippa,
From Scenes of Palestine,
To Memory,

AMUSEMENTS OF SOLITUDE

Verses to Guthrie Castle.

"What strong mysterious links enchain the heart
To regions where the morn of life was spent!"
                                    GRAHAME.

I.

YET o'er thy ivied walls what eye can skance,

Nor feel deep thought enwrap the soul ?[1] Thus stand

In gloom of years, which saw thy turrets glance

As hostile to the hostile of thy land.

Proud stream'd thy banners o'er thy trusty band,

Taught foes to feed the dust whereon they breath'd;

Or, slaughter 'scap'd, they woo'd the briny strand,

And rueful told how they in Scotia skaith'd,

And what might hap, ere with the Rose the Thistle wreath'd.

VERSES TO GUTHRIE CASTLE

II.

Peace to the spirits of thy martial sons,

For of thy lineage these the crimson tide

That flowed on **Flowden**, sweeping from thy loins,

The root and scion of thy nation's pride![2]

Cried not the plover from thy mountain side?

Screech'd not the owl when flitting thro' thy bowers?[3]

That sable drapery would thy hopes deride,

And cloud the halo of thy brighter hours

In grief that weeps not, speaks not, yet the heart o'erpowers.

III.

And these are of thee still;[4] long may it boast

An arm to strengthen freedom, and to check

The torrent of invaders on our coast,

Who only breathe to build on freedom's wreck.

Still may thy name and lineage claim respect

From grateful country, or her chequer'd page,

And from your halls the happy sounds awake

That hallow time, cleave to the precepts sage

Which point to brighter skies - a purchased heritage

VERSES TO GUTHRIE CASTLE

IV.

And whilst I write, is there not tun'd the tongue,

Speaks mirth to youth, and strives age to beguile,[5]

From sunny skies where Petrarch sweetly sung,

A lady-fair hies to our northern isle.

Why hang her eyes upon the love- lit smile

Beams from yon scion by the altar side?

O, ask not! Lady-love stands pledged erewhile,

And he has vow'd to take her for his bride.

O, may their bark glide smoothly down life's chafed tide!

V.

And Scotland's sons have warmly knit the band

That claims the daughter of our sea-born isle.

Her maidens, too, haste with the heart and hand

To peal a welcome with a sister's smile.

And will not such from youth's remembrance wile

Of legends dear, a mother's fondness wrote,

The hallow'd home of days unknown to guile,

Each well-known face, where eye conveyed thought,

And spoke the prized wish, - say, are these all forgot?

VERSES TO GUTHRIE CASTLE

VI.

Ah, no! The mind will win its way and fondly glide

To other climes, and sounds of early morn

Will break their echo on the flowing tide

The heart cannot suppress, though pleasure borne,

And o'er such feelings sweep the world in scorn,

Nor deigns a balm the wound to mollify,

Till time, with heavy wings, has smoother worn

Each keener edge of mortal destiny,

And deeply schools the heart with more than worlds can buy.

VII.

And I have lov'd thee well. Ere surging life

Had launch'd my shallop on its angry foam,

And traced upon my brow the saddening strife

Speaks pain and sleepless hours, I lov'd to roam

Around thy bowers, claim thee my bosom home;

Nor yet the picture lost though paths untrod,

My heart yet speaks, in nature's vivid tome,

To each grey stone and tree, each lov'd abode,

Where careless boyhood slumber'd on its thoughtless road.

VERSES TO GUTHRIE CASTLE

VIII.

The brook that murmurs by, the daisied lawn,

The birken-mingled copse, which o'er the waste

Breathes fragrance on the breeze, when twinkling dawn

Hangs pearly dew- drops on her balmy breast:

And low in nature's kingdom, but not least

To please her lovers, is the wild bee's hum;

The tuneless butterfly so gaudy drest,

Who joys to see her short - liv'd day is come,

Nor dreams to- morrow's sun shines on her early tomb.

IX.

The Lunan murmurs on its soothing voice,

The daizied lawn still glints to nature's smile,

And from the woodland feather'd tribes rejoice

When morning dawns, and evening quits her toil;

And these will gladden hearts, and serve to wile

From heavy hours, as they have gladden'd mine.

When but a few more seasons round shall while,

My pen shall heedless drop, and memory's shrine

In fragments lie, that used to tell of me or mine.

NOTES

ON

VERSES TO GUTHRIE CASTLE

Note 1, Verse 1.

" Yet o'er thy ivied walls what eye can skance,
Nor feel deep thought enwrap the soul? "

In the year 1468, Sir David Guthrie had a Royal warrant under the great seal for building the tower and castle of Guthrie, and, subsequently resigning the barony of Guthrie into the king's hand, he obtained a new charter converting the tenure from Ward to Blench, holding of the king for payment of one penny silver Scots money, at the principal manor- place of Guthrie, in name of Blench Farm, if asked allenarly. This charter is dated 12th February, 1470, and bears to have been granted as a recompence for his faithful services, and for the singular favour which the king bore to him. He filled successively the honourable and highly responsible situations of Armour-bearer to King James III, lord -treasurer of Scotland, comptroller of the exchequer, lord registrar of Scotland, and lord of the exchequer, lord registrar of Scotland, and lord chief justice of Scotland.

NOTES ON VERSES

He founded and endowed a collegiate church at Guthrie, 1479. He married a daughter of Sir Thomas Maule, lord of Panmure.

Note 2, Verse 2.
" The crimson tide
That flowed on Flowden, sweeping from thy loins
The root and scion of thy nation's prid."

Sir Alexander Guthrie, surrounded by friends and vassals, attended his sovereign to the fatal field of Flowden, and there fell (9th Sept. 1513), with his eldest son David, his three brothers-in-law - David, William, and George Lyon - and his nephew, Sir Thomas Maule of Panmure.

Note 3, Verse 2.
" Cried not the plover from thy mountain side?
Screech'd not the owl when flitting thro' thy bowers? "

Alluding to the superstition of the period when these were regarded as birds of bad omen. Such is not altogether yet extinct in Scotland.

Note 4, verse 3.
" And these are of thee still. "

Captain William Guthrie, presently an officer in the 42d regiment.

TO GUTHRIE CASTLE.

Note 5, Verse 4.

"And whilst I write, is there not tun'd the tongue
Speaks mirth to youth, and strives age to beguile?"

At the time these verses were being wrote, John Guthrie, Esq. younger of Guthrie, was married to a lady of Leghorn, Italy, July 23, 1844.

The Maid of the Valley, a Dream.
WITH NOTES.

" In earlier days and calmer hours,
When heart with heart delights to blend ,
Where bloom my native valley's bowers ,
I had-ah ! have I now ?-a friend."

BYRON.

CONTENTS .

A Coincidence. — A Parting Scene. —Sorrows attending on such. - A Highland Scene and Sunny Glen. Of the heart's attachment to nativity, never altogether effaced. - Revisited in Dreams assuages Captivity and the Exile. Sportive Feats of Light Hearts. — A Pensive Damsel. A párting farewell is wrote on her hear. -Her fingers beat time. - The aching of the heart under such. - Long in being effaced. - Digression on Innate Philosophy; it nerves the Patriot and the Martyr. The workings of fancy on a retrospection. The vision breaks, and the heart feels it all a fragment from the page of early life. - The Valley G"". The winding stream L ""

THE MAID OF THE VALLEY.

I.

AH me! to sing the workings undefin'd

That move to strength this free, yet captive sweet,

The unembodied floatings of the mind,

The flight of language, and the glance complete

Electric shock, the unperceived bind,

The feast of hope with sighs, and fears replete,

Would lead my nursling to a wild unknown,

Or known 'twas early, and now haply flown.

II.

'Tis even: melts on mine ear the mavis' song:

I heard it then-methinks she has not flit;

And lapse of wintry years I recked long

Does swell a dream, and now my fancy's lit.

And meet I yet the searching lustring hit,

The silver'd voice of love's heart-wending throe? [1]

And by my side does all I liv'd for sit?

I'll fold thy form, deep surge my fabled woe,

Deem'd almost sterile truth, and say-but oh!

THE MAID OF THE VALLEY.

III.

My hopes were warm, and far outran the growth

Of sapient acts, for then I was a boy.

And then upon the vision of my youth

Where fell a mildew, damping to my joy:

I stood beneath a yew- tree with the cloy

Of thwarted wishes-felt a chill'd adieu

Wrench'd from a phantom of the heart-a toy

That verged into thought, and from it drew

A long, long saddening sigh, when joys were few.

IV.

A change came o'er my dream: I stray'd alone,

Where heath and rocks were nature's garnitude;[2]

On either hand was hung the hoary frown

Of valley-darkening cliffs. 'Twas solitude,

Save when the eagle to her rock borne brood,

With dusky pinions, sweep'd the speckless blue-

Save when some knitless fragment left the rude

Unshapen mass, and down the diggy brow

Responsive caverns rung repeating echoes through.

THE MAID OF THE VALLEY.

V.

A sunny glen out spangling to the west,

And homes of industry, broke on my view;

Clear was the rivulet, and its dimpling breast

Invers'd the placid welkin's deepening blue;

The birk, the blossom'd briar, the cowslip, threw

Their fragrance, mingled with the mountain thyme; -

It was a scene to such the heart's adieu

Responds no echo, though the wings of time

May bid us print strange lands inhale another clime.[3]

VI.

Well known the notes that melted on my ear

From upland thickets of the winding stream,

And oft the village song I us'd to hear,

To lovers' hearts it spoke a tender theme:

In love I felt it not, yet had it claim

Upon my heart. I, melancholy, mus'd

With far-fetched thought, as in the guiling dream

The captive to his freedom is arous'd,

The drooping exile hails the scenes his heart has choos'd.[4]

THE MAID OF THE VALLEY.

VII.

And O! methought the village youngsters tripp'd,

With lightsome heart, life's morning giddy maze,

And pleasure shone on cheeks that seem'd as dipp'd

With roseate dye, each whiled their devious ways

(Such as I'd mingl'd with in other days),

In rustic sports, though wild, yet not uncouth.

Each youthful maiden caught the blushing praise

Was warded on her feats with lovers sooth,

And each breast beat the happy, thoughtless joys of youth.

VIII.

But there was one who mingled not the heart,

Nor to the buoyant portion lent a smile,

Deep was the thought that swath'd her breast, and part

Sat on her brow, whom mirth could not beguile.

All in a bower she sat within a pile

Of fissur'd rocks, where echo loves to dwell,

And o'er a kerchief did she, sighing, while

The weary moments of her bosom swell,

And wrought the heart-corroding word - Farewell, farewell

THE MAID OF THE VALLEY.

IX.

And from her raven locks she drew the thread

That knit the emption of her love and care.

Methought 'twas wayward; for the baneful weed

Had sprung to life-sown desolation there.

'Tis not that nature blooms so fresh and fair

The face is taught to dimple into joy,

Nor when she mourns her fields of beauties bare

The eye is prompt'd to tears; - within's the buoy

That bears us on to bliss, the bliss we deem is coy.

X.

Within's the gangrene that may fret the soul,

Though all around has caught the ruddy beam;

Within may joy arise, though round us toll

The chime of woe, until the knell grow tame,

Whence springs the peace that gilds the bleeding name

The patriot spurns not, nor the martyr mourns.

Such to a higher birth-place has a claim

Than ours, which on a mortal axis turns,

Whose flickering breath feels cold from flattery's marbl'd urns.

THE MAID OF THE VALLEY.

XI.

And she would muse on such, and silent seem

To hold a converse with the far away,[6]

To parted hearts more than the reckless deem

Is garner'd in the simple farewell say:

O'er what has been will lingering memory stray,

And plighted faith unblighted gild the gloom;

A word, a look, a fancied grasp will play

What erst it play'd, and dew the languid bloom;

These are the treasur'd of the heart, the soul's illume.

XII.

And these may wrap whom fortune reckless cleft,

But cleft in love, in hope to meet again;

But far, far other is whom she has reft

From each, and doom'd them ever to be twain:

Each thought is woe, each sigh a bursting pain,

Brief is their pleasure and their sadness all,

The turmoil of the world o'erwhelms in vain

To quench the past, and wintry years may fall

Man's bounded age, ere from love's blight he all recall.

THE MAID OF THE VALLEY.

XIII.

And oft to ward the thoughtless vacant jeer

A smile will wither where a tear would grow;[7]

Even from ourselves we with the thoughtless steer,

And leave a mass of heart-condensed woe,

Swift skims the spirit to the Upas blow;

The transient mingling seems delusion's play,

A borrowed lustre in the shade to glow,

And what has been, a sigh, a tear may say,

A withered smile may mark the weary plodded way.

XIV.

My spirit, whither dost thou wander? She,

The valley maiden, lags and weeps behind.

Why weeps she? Wild winds sweep as wantonly

The tender floweret as the mountain pine.

We slip the reins, delusion cheats the mind,

We sleep the sleep conceives our very tears,

And all our joys a flimsy dream combin'd,

Whose evanescence congregates our fears,

And stamps the heart and face with more than number'd years.

THE MAID OF THE VALLEY.

XV.

Fair maiden, weep not; was there not a tear

That twinkled in the orbs of crushed love,

A gem of sorrow to my heart was dear,

And rous'd a latency no words could move?

Nor 'yond this maiden could I further rove.

She sat the pillow of my spirit's rest,

And as the growing word her needle wove

She oftentimes would pause, then ply in haste,

As grief, or flattering hope, did fluctuate her breast.

XVI.

She look'd not on me, and my spirit caught

The chilly canker of neglectfulness;[8]

I grasped her hand and sighed, for I was taught

Beyond control her bosom's deep express:

The vision fled, my spirit, actionless,

Hung as a vapour o'er inanity,

The willing dupe of its own waywardness,

And morning wak'd me, yet I pondered why

So much of waking life within a dream did lie.

THE MAID OF THE VALLEY.

XVII.

The scene is fled: it was enchantment's wand,

A sweet delusion of the waking eye; -

'Twas as a feature from the fairy land,

The scenes of silent life we nightly nigh; -

'Twas as a foot-print on the livid sand,

The lap of rolling waves; - 'twas as the sky,

Blush deep confusion, gild the rugged steep,

Prelusive that the coming day will weep.

XVIII.

Such was the valley, such the winding stream,

Where I was wont to while my youth away;

Such was the maiden of my feeling dream

First taught me love.

NOTES
TO
THE MAID OF THE VALLEY

Note I, Verse 2.

"And meet I yet the searching lustring hit,
The silver'd voice of love's heart- rending throe"

Love, thou sweet, yet bitter-mingled passion, thou magnet betwixt hope and disappointment, how dost thou fold the soul in ethereal bliss, when thou teachest her to expand her beauties to thy fair blown blossom, e'en the fairest that adorn the human breast. ! wax not cold to diem that anticipate thee, that feasts, yet unfeasted, in thy chaste embraces, when the sober arms of twilight is grasping to all, saw them, a weary world; nor flee from the heart that, over the shrine of Hymen, has vowed to cherish thy eluding form. Man, unconscious man, in the fever of youth, knows not the capability of his heart: fond, youthful hearts love on, but dare not to ask the fruition or every hope, lest the surcharged heart should ask where is pleasure.

NOTES TO THE MAID OF THE VALLEY.

Note 2, Verse 4.

" I strayed alone
Where heath and rocks were nature's garnitude. "

I am afraid too little of nature's grandeur, such as the Highlands of Scotland present, has fallen to my view, for awakening ideas true to nature. There is an innate painting of the mind which will go a great way; but it is as the outlines of a well conceived picture-travelling stores the mind with imagery which can only fill it up. Beattie's Minstrel is much in unison with my heart in describing mountain scenery, and its effects on the poetic mind: " Lo, where the stripling wrapt," & c.

Note 3, Verse 6.

" The heart's adieu
Responds no echo, though the wings of time
May bid us print strange lands-inhale another clime."

The heart is tenacious of the spot that gave us birth, even though its scenery should beam forth in a dream. We cannot satisfactorily account for these feelings. The tender bark is etched with some favourite name, and the impression expands as the tree gains growth. Such feelings require not the refinements of life to nurse them, they are evidently the language of nature. The rough untutored mountaineer of our own. land loves his blue hills, and, as the lichens of his native pine, his heart grasps at the barren rock where his feet

NOTES TO THE MAID OF THE VALLEY.

first learned to wander; and, barren rock though it be, he only leaves it when oppression refuses him shelter, and on some lone height his farewell is breathed with the melancholy strains of his pibroch. Does the dingy African pine for the sunny soil and Mangoe groves that gave him birth? Alas! the reproachful annals of nations can tell he does. The Grecian girl on the Moslem slave-mart weeps for the mother she never more may behold, and clasps the fragments of her finery to her breast, as the remembrance of some dear loved spot.

Note 4, Verse 7.

"As in the guiling dream
The captive to his freedom is aroused,
The drooping exile hails the scenes his heart has choos'd. "

Dreaming is a faculty of the soul that yields not to fetters or distance. The captive drooping in his dungeon catches a respite from his sorrows; and the exile, far from the loved haunts of infancy, can mingle again with the friends of his youth. There is a certain class who, clinging fast to the dark sayings of other days, regard dreams with a superstitious awe. I view them not through that channel, for my mind is not tenacious of these things; and yet dreams, divested of superstition, wear a charm that I cannot altogether

NOTES TO THE MAID OF THE VALLEY.

lay aside ;-I love to indulge in presentiment. That may be a weakness, - I had almost said a presumption, nay, I am convinced it is one, - but we often err against conviction. Some dreams have been mine that have borne a remarkable coincidence to what has befallen me.

Note 6, Verse 12.
"And she would muse on such, and silent seem
To hold a converse with the far away."

There is a soothing pleasure in hope which the sterility of life chases away; and such is the human heart, that even the fruition of that hope which lies nearest our heart falls far short of the visionary beam. The fact is, we live more by shadow than substance. The mother presseth the aching brow of her darling infant to her own. True, the fears of her heart have stolen the roses from her cheeks. But mark her eye! Is there not a lustre that beameth through her sorrows, and the sweet voice of hope whispereth in her heart that sickness may not be unto death. What giveth the heart that serenity and peace when the storms of adversity lowers thick around? Adversity is not always misery; and although wind and wave may assail without, the heart, anchored within herself, sees a country whose cloudless skies never witnessed a tear, and the sweet voice of hope bids her persevere; it is her home, when the trammels of mortality

NOTES TO THE MAID OF THE VALLEY.

are laid aside. Such are some of the pleasures which hope inspireth, and I doubt not the experience of life will give sanction to what I have advanced.

Note 5, Verse 8.
"And each breast beat the happy thoughtless joys of youth."

We look on the rose: one thought admires it, and the next mourns that such beauty should mingle with the dust.

> "At morn a dew- bath'd rose I past,
> All lovely on its native stalk,
> Unmindful of the noonday blast,
> That strew'd it on my evening walk."

I hope Menelaus will excuse me for taking a handful of his copyright, it is a beautiful idea. Even so it is with youth: its buoyant heart dreams not of the stern rigidity of years; indulging in a retrospective view, perhaps there is no time which imparts us so much pleasure as that period of giddy years. There may be some parts of the best spent lives that will not brook a look, and undoubtedly much that yields regret. Such we would fondly recall, not to act anew, but more wisely; but if we wish for the innocent days of youth again, it is to act the same giddy round-to clasp to our breasts the same, and the only portion of life, which leaves no sting, whilst we sip the honey unalloyed.

NOTES TO THE MAID OF THE VALLEY.

Note 7, Verse 14.

*"And oft to ward the thoughtless vacant jeer,
A smile will wither where a tear would grow."*

We judge from appearances ; and the face that can smile is often deemed the index of a happy heart . But let our thoughts turn to ourselves, and the heart will unfold another tale. Every passion is capable of affectation; but art is known from nature. The chalice of palling pleasure is drained, and the reckless bustle of the crowd is alike resorted to, to save us from ourselves. Perhaps there is no enemy equal in power to self. From the bite of envy, and the scorn of the malignant, an asylum is found in our consciousness; but how can we look on the smiling breast? That is probably a strong character; but I am persuaded society has many such; -every breast feels what cannot, and dare not, find a tongue.

Note 8, Verse 17.

" The chilling canker of neglectfulness. "

What we deem trifles often appear of importance to those we come in contact with. Thus the chilling canker is strongly displayed in overlooking what demanded our attention. Love has died away, friendship has found a tomb, and correspondence, blooming from congenial hearts, has withered over the embers that a simple reply could have fanned into flames.

A Legend of Mull

> " There never yet was human power
> Who could evade, if unforgiven,
> The patient search and vigil long
> Of him who treasures up a wrong."
>
> BYRON.

THE name of Benin Gorod, in Mull, a mountain with bassaltes pillars 200 feet in height, discovered by Mr Raspe in the year 1789, and far superior to Staffa, the Giant's Causeway, or any other specimen of the kind hitherto known, arises from a story of a nature so truly tragical, that it merits to be preserved. There are many traditions respecting it, but the following seems to be the most authentic. Mackinnon, a powerful chieftain, was lord of the island many years ago. He was no less distinguished for the extent of his territories, where he resided in great feudal magnificence, than for a ferocity of temper which knew no bounds, and a spirit of avarice which he found no means of satisfying, but by grievously oppressing his tenants and

A LEGEND OF MULL.

vassals, and seizing their property and estates. He was particularly anxious to acquire the possession of a chieftain of lesser degree whose name was Gorod, on account of the extent and contiguity, but had long abstained from any attempt of the kind, both as Gorod, though above fifty years of age, had remained unmarried, and, failing of him and his heirs, the estate reverted to the chieftain, and because his only son was reared, according to the custom of the times, in the family of a vassal, was in his custody. Gorod, however, contrary to the expectation of every one, married a young lady of great beauty and accomplishments, whom he had accidentally met with in one of the neighbouring islands, and the chieftain had reason to apprehend that the expectations with which he had flattered himself of getting his vassal's estate by a failure of his posterity would be frustrated. Impelled by lust and disappointment, he resolved to destroy the hopes and happiness of Gorod by seducing his wife, which he with difficulty effected, and at last carried her in triumph to Castle Aros.

Gorod concealed his rage, whilst he inwardly vowed vengeance; and having contrived, in the course of a great hunting party, at which the chieftain and his son, Gorod and the lady, and all the principal people of the island assisted, to bring the whole company to the summit of a very lofty mountain, he seized the youth, and standing on the brink of

A LEGEND OF MULL.

frightful precipice, exclaimed." This instant I plunge myself and this boy down the cliff unless that infamous woman is put to death by the hands of her seducer. " The chieftain, trembling for the only support of his family, and encouraged by the persuasions of his unhappy mistress, who presented her breast to receive the stroke, reluctantly obeyed. Gorod then cried out, " I am revenged, but that tyrant must be punished;" then springing from the mountain with the unhappy youth in his arms, they were almost instantly dashed to pieces. The place has ever since been known by the name of Benin Gorod, or the Hill of Gorod; and the prospect from its summit excites a degree of horror which it is impossible to describe.

INTRODUCTORY LINES.

THE serfs in Mull wear in their breasts

The plant of peace their lord has not;

Their humble fare is 'yond his feasts;

His mocking halls yield not their lot.

And why? The tale is deep and long,

Nor poet's lay, nor minstrel's song

A LEGEND OF MULL.

E're compass'd it: it barely shone

Upon the page long lost and gone.

Tradition dar'd time to outbrave,

And snatch'd it from oblivion's grave.

Through ages past it roll'd along,

Until my ear received the chime,

And weaving it in artless song,

Has woo'd the barbs from lagging time.

Thus far I've known the sweets of life-

Thus far I've solace woo'd when cheerless-

I've pleased myself, not having wife;

For pleasing others I am careless.

Methinks, were I to specify

The reasons of this heart indifference,

My foes perchance might multiply

Beyond the limits of a preference.

'Tis well for men that they have foes,

Such is the ballast in life's ocean;

But then beyond enough's a noose,

A trammel for each noble notion.

A LEGEND OF MULL.

'Twere well, 'twere wise, could mankind guide

The heart to meet life's varying measure-

'Twould many heartaches save, beside

Remorse, that ruthless tax on pleasure.

A LEGEND OF MULL.

Time - a little before Sunset.

THE chase is o'er - the huntsmen rest

On Benmore's height, whose craggy breast

O'erhangs the blue unfathom'd wide,

Wild chaffings of a ceaselsss tide.

The chase is o'er-the placid eve

Soft mellows over earth and wave,

And, stretching wide in glittering smile,

Enthron'd on waves, sits rock and isle:

Iona, Staffa, Colonsa,

Fling back the glance through ocean's spray,

And Scarba's rocks, and Jura's peaks,

From valley pass, and mountain breaks

A LEGEND OF MULL.

Dip in the glance; low round the base

Loch Scridan's wave its music plays;

'Neath shelvy rock, and craggy steep,

The sea fowls bold unyielding keep,

Through caverns wild they fret and hiss

Their lashing froth o'er wave's abyss.

The chase is o'er-the game's unscaith'd,

But vengeance' sword is now unsheath'd,

And Gorod overhangs the steep,

And in his arms is seen to weep

A youth; and down his downy cheek

The big sweat rolls; but he is meek,

And scarcely writhes: they verge on death,

And view its portals underneath:

One fatal step, and all is gone;

One fleeting breath one parting groan -

One dashing echo from the steep,

And hovering ravens mark the spot -

The crimson-stain'd - the dreamless sleep,

And one's life-weary - one is not,

A LEGEND OF MULL.

And oh! on Gorod he does brook

The meaning of a dying look,

That fain would live; but he, in spite,

O'er looks the look with one, nor bright,

Nor cloudy, but a fiendish shone

Of treasur'd vengeance for the gone.

So will the fleecy victim scan

Death, whetted on the ruthless knife;

And, shrinking, feel the stubborn hand

Search for the vein of vital life.

Another look to mercy 'gain

Vain pleads thy heart: the knitted e'e,

Unmoved, says mercy pleads in vain,

And thou art what thou fear'd to be.

   He pauses. Yet they may recall.

He waves his kerchief to the crowd:

His accents fell: to one they fall

As death, though from the brink he stood

In farthest way; and who is he?

Why clasps his hands across his breast?

A LEGEND OF MULL.

And why in wild rapidity

His eye-balls roll? -they deem the test

Of senses flown-of anguish deep-

The wake of what shall never sleep.

Such is Mackinnon. Then 'tis he.

And wherefore so? Upon the brink

His son does live, but soon may be

A thing the living fear to think.

So Gorod has Mackinnon's son.

Ah me! the youth with downy cheek,

His brooding spirit here has run,

For fell revenge, now 'bout to wreak,

And Aros' house will fade to nought,

Its only scion's in Gorod's grasp,

A craggy grave is doom'd his lot.

His father sees, and one does not,

Nor ere again her form he'll clasp.

O! linger fame, nor haste to tell

Where sleeps what once she loved well;

Haste not to deck in weeds of woe

A LEGEND OF MULL.

The breast that hoards a parting kiss,

That fond will dream it wert not so,

And chides the morn that rives her bliss.

Zelica, daughter of the chief

Of Kilda's isle, prolong your smile,

Nor chide the wave that tards the skiff

Of all you lov'd from yon green isle.

Unveil, and veil your lattice high,

No moon-beam dances on the wave;

Perchance your well-known lights descry,

Will light a wanderer, cheer the brave.

Cause maidens spread your bridal bed,

Soft shake the down to soothe your head.

Why soothe your head? Will cypress weave?

Will pain cause wedlock's bosom heave?

The fell owl screams, - ah me! she hears, -

Her bosom nurses gathering fears!

And Gorod speaks: - " This moment I,

This youth you love - I care not - die.

A LEGEND OF MULL.

Long ills I've borne - long swath'd in grief

This bosom's bled. Now, haughty chief,

Though stole the diadem from my breast,

Know here revenge can find relief,

And o'er your feelings whet to feast.

I Anna lov'd; -but that is gone;

I wed her ' cause she loved me.

But woman's wiles will dim the shone

Of virtue; and the past to me

Has gender'd hell, where peace should be.

Now let the guilty 'tone for guilt,

Mackinnon's sword in Anna's breast:

Thence sprang his love, thence I have felt

What now I feel. " They speak the rest.

Hope, in Mackinnon's eye, forlorn

Thou sat-thou sit'st; the breast is torn,

The thirsty sword's in blood arrayed

Once warm'd the lov'd, and loving stray'd,

Flows fast the stream of life, and drench'd

With clotting gore's the waving grass;

A LEGEND OF MULL.

The glazed eye, the stubborn clench'd,

Of agony marks the pregnant pass,

And Anna's spirit's far away,

Fleet as the morning's ambient ray,

(If pen dare measure spirit's flight)

To regions of eternal light,

Unseen as zephyr on the wave

That crinkles o'er the dreamless brave.

And shrink'd her heart to meet the steel?

O no! her breast was op'd to heal

A wound that rankl'd in a heart

She knew, she felt for, and to part

With life, this last dear sacrifice,

She deem'd as nought, if 'twould suffice.

And when the steel would search for life,

She tore the kerchief well, I ween.

'Twas Mackinnon's once; he gaz'd with grief,

Nor to o'erlooked he felt relief.

It whisper'd what should never been.

So yields the heart when tempests boil

A LEGEND OF MULL.

Their fury o'er man's puny toil.

The bark is lighten'd, on the wave

Is strew'd the gifts that fortune gave,

In hostage tender'd; but in vain,

The thankless deep the gifts retain,

Nor lists the call would plead for life,

Wave meets o'er wave in maddening strife.

   The deed is done. The stern command,

If not with hearts obey'd, with hand,

And fondly feeling hope would dare

To pinion still a father's prayer.

The silence breaks, the fragile thread

Hangs on the fiat; with breathless greed

The draught is quaff'd.

" Yet from the shade that film your eyes

A ray of hope you think will rise;

But, haughty chief, know there is none.

There is but one on whom I frown:

That form is thine: not on the crowd,

A LEGEND OF MULL.

Not on this boy my thoughts be rude;

But sparing him were sparing thee;

And much I've spared, much I've felt;

So he, the sapling of the tree,

Must quench the torrent of your guilt. "

They near the verge, and underneath,

"Twixt them and death's one parting breath,

Is all between, and more than all,

One grasps the grasp of death - they fall.

The chase is o'er: Sun's setting light

Stream'd calmly over Benmore's height,

And bade adieu to tower and tree,

'Midst strains of woodland minstrelsy.

The chase is o'er, the game is caught,

A father's drunk a bitter draught.

The far- fetch'd price of joys impure

Lay, serpent- coil'd, in lover's bower,

Now deathless stings his every hour.

A LEGEND OF MULL.

Sleep on, thou chieftain of a race,

Wast not the worst, though goaded on

To turn thy hand to gain the peace

Another's from thee basely won.

Slow is the hand of minstrelsy

To spread a halo round his doom,

Slow swells the strains to memory

That us'd to grace a chieftain's tomb.

The heaving surge his dirge shall sing, -

It pictures well his troubled mind;

The sea fowl, on her flapping wing,

His deeds shall echo to the wind.

Sleep on, thou chieftain! low thy bed,

And dank the pillow ' neath thy head.

Thou wert not cynic, but thy heart

Lov'd much to breathe a cynic's creed,

And o'er life's sympathising part

It hurried on in haughty speed;

Yet not for these too much to blame,

Thus only haughty in the crowd,

A LEGEND OF MULL.

Whose overcoming eye would shame

To seem'd indifference traits of good.

Thine was the eye that flitted by,

Yet deep, perceiveless was its prey.

The cheek was thine; the gather'd brow

No social wiles could e'er subdue;

For well thy ' volving mind could scan,

And deeply read the map of man;

But of his name, his deeds, or doom,

Beyond this page there is no trace:

His body rests in ocean's tomb,

His spirit who dare say her place!

The Bride of Lismore

IN TWO PARTS.

PART FIRST

"Ah! were I sever'd from thy side
Who were my friend, and who thy guide?
Years have not seen, time shall not see,
The hour that tears my soul from thee."

BYRON.

CONTENTS.

A Spring Morning. - The Minstrel's Song. - The Listening Heroine. Digression on Choice, on Thought. - Effects of Music on the Ear and Heart. - On Echo : Contrast of the Memory with Echo ; Effect of the Minstrel's Song on the Maiden ; a Call to Awaken ; the Morning Bell ; Her Solitude and Phrensy occasioned thereby , shown by her neglected Flowers , &c . The Isle of Pines. - A Piratical Nest: Description of such. - In a Westward Voyage, they rescue Edwin, on the night of his peril, when going to see his Bride. The Captain's Daughter: Description of her,

THE BRIDE OF LISMORE

of her twin brother and Saxon mother, of a Western Churchyard. -Digression on such. The Corsair's Daughter fails to gain the heart of Edwin. - He pants to return home. —Digression on attachment to the Land of our Birth. - Edwin thrills on a chord of the Captain's early days. His return is permitted. He visits his Island Maiden. — She sleeps by the shore wave. She dreams of him. - She awakens and realises the same,

> And the joy that's bled for, the sweetest, the best,
> Its halo shall shed o'er the hopes of his breast.

'Tis morning breaks upon the sullen brow

Of yon cliff- hanging steep, the ambient flood,

And blends his beauties o'er the gilded view

Of rock and glen, and upland solitude.

Sweet hour of cradled woe, to your intrude

My heart wafts welcome, and I haste to roam

To sip your sweets, unknown to deemed good,

   Who press the down, and they who strew the bloom

Of manhood o'er the grape, the morrow's torched tomb.

THE BRIDE OF LISMORE

    The virent mead, the daisy-spotted lawn,
    The breathless stage, the scene of jocund feats.
    Soft miniature of life, how aptly drawn!
    Its eager, vain pursuits-its dire defeats;
    The upland sloping lea, the lambkin bleats;
    The brook we pleasing trac'd, when dewy morn
    Sat listing, luring from their perch'd retreats
    The linnet, thrush, each of the groves adorn,
And they who trill their songs through fields of ether borne.

    Light wheels the swallow through the ocean spray;
    Sweet down the vale the cuckoo's note is heard;
    The dew-drop yields unto the thirsty sway
    Of morning splendour from the balmy sward.
    Sweet on the gale is borne the meet reward
    Of nature's offspring unto nature's King.
    O, sweet the spring! and Lismore's isle appear'd
    A lily on the waste; or saintly sing
Of heavenly anchor'd peace, where earth's commotions ring.

THE BRIDE OF LISMORE

All in a cliffy nook, where morning stray'd

In hafflin splendour, sat a minstrel hoar:

His bronzed locks light to the zephyrs play'd;

His garb was plain, and such as minstrels wore.

O, sat he there to list the dashing roar

Of circumambient waves in tameless play?

Why fasts his eyes upon another shore?

'Tis meditation. See, he's strung to say

With harp, where glides his soul to earth or heaven's obey.

SONG OF THE MINSTREL.

"A youth to Lismore's isle yestreen

Hung o'er his boat prow, wan and weary:

The thunder's roll and lightening's sheen

Forbade his loving heart be cheery.

And as he rode the chaffed waves,

The mermaid rose, and sung before him

The song of woe, whilst echoing caves

Hung thick the wrath that gather'd o'er him.

Row, boatman, row! thy lamp of life

THE BRIDE OF LISMORE

Expands the bloom in beauty's bosom.

Row, boatman, row! and brave the strife,

Let hopes on distant days repose them.

His mother waited in her hall,

And looked from her lattice dreary,

And ever and anon her call

Was, " Edwin, O! how long you tarry! "

Well ween'd her heart the path was short

That row'd atween him and his deary;

But ah! she little ween'd his heart

Against the storm was waxing weary.

Faint was her heart, and fainter still,

As twinkling dawn proclaim'd the morrow,

And as they valley sought and hill,

It thicker weav'd her web of sorrow.

And now for faded hopes there's weeds,

The weeds that mantle in the bosom.

The virent heart but briefly bleeds,

But ah! the aged's loath to lose them. "

The minstrel paused, and heaved his breast:

THE BRIDE OF LISMORE

I ween that grief became his guest.

The minstrel paused, and there were tears

Stole down the furrows of his years.

I trow ' twas deep he felt and sung.

Now deeply silence seal'd his tongue;

Then, as if nerv'd anew, to tell

Prophetic from some oracle,

He strung anew, and thrid along

The mystic meaning of his song:

THE MINSTREL'S SONG CONTINUED.

"My lady shall weep, my lady shall sigh;

But sorrows shall sleep, and tears they will dry,

When from the fair west, the bright star of eve

Shall beam on the crest of the loving and brave.

Whilst over the ocean he heaves the deep sigh

That speaks the emotion of what is gone by,

To the isle of his sires, the isle of the brave,

Hope conquers his fears, he parts the green wave;

And the joy that's bled for, the sweetest, the best,

Its halo shall shed o'er the hopes of his breast."

THE BRIDE OF LISMORE

On Lake Etive fair Helen laves

Her tiny vessel with the wave.

Such was her morning's wonted ply.

There would she mark the closing day, -

There, Lake Etive, thy rippling crest

Soft mellowed the tender song, -

There was the lisping tale confest

Dreams not that patience deems it long.

Another's arm has plied the oar,

Another's voice has tender sung,

Another's look has glanced o'er

The face, where yielding sweetness hung.

O! who can mark the growth of love,

Or say from whence it subtle springs?

A sigh - a glance - the texture's wove,

And all of fancy lends it wings.

The speechless moments vast express,

When kindred hands together strain,

The cunning tongue may well say less,

But more but this is all in vain

THE BRIDE OF LISMORE

Dear is the form we centre all

We deem of earth, and hinge the heart;

Yet only may the sweet enthrall

Be ours - be ours the woe to part.

'Tis not that features form the bind,

Though features may adorn the choice,

Love drinks the subtle of the mind,

And thought in thought concentrate joys.

Oh! what is thought?   A fleeting thing

Whereon a tear, a smile will wing

Our often more than bodied ill -

The bane or balm of every will -

The death, the life, the more than we

Can gather from the passing round -

The glean of earth, of air, and sea,

Man's only thing that knows no bound.

  And from the craggy shore is borne

The minstrel's song in distance worn.

Light skimming o'er the rippling lake,

It melted on the maiden's ear.

THE BRIDE OF LISMORE

O! sweet the theme, it seem'd to wake;

The prow is turn'd the bank to near.

She fix'd her eyes upon the shore

As if the minstrel to descry,

And pausing, plied the guiding oar

In careless mood - so listenly.

There is in such a heavenly sound

That gathers on the list'ing soul,

As if the intervening ground

Lent magic to its sweet control.

We list, and list, nor can we turn;

E'en misery quits her sable chair;

And grief, suspended, leaves her urn,

And half forgets what makes it dear.

The tear that wins away by stealth

From beauty's eyes will pleasure sip

From lingering on the cheek, and wreathe

As dew drops on the rose's lip.

   The minstrel ceased: the passing note

Rode on the breeze that freshen'd morn,

THE BRIDE OF LISMORE

Soft tingling on the airy float,

It waken'd echo's mellow horn:

Now round the rock, now in the spray,

It mingles with the dashing roar

In soft vibrations - brief its stay -

It glides away-'tis now no more.

There is a pleasure thus to hear,

And hearing, know not whence ' tis found:

'Tis the mystic agent to the ear

Of what was spoke - is breath'd to sound.

Deep in the glen it loves to wend

Its airy form, where silence bend

Out o'er the antique sylvan bower -

Where naiads revel - where the hour

Of noontide shoots a mystic gray;

And high o'er head the pine trees play,

Whose lichens hoop the fissur'd pile

Of moss-clad rocks that hem the file

Of aerial march, and aerial dance,

At least supported in romance.

THE BRIDE OF LISMORE

Thou echo in thy wildest wind

Of what is past, remindest me

Of one, the deeper of the mind

We feel, we term the memory.

Deep in the burrows of the heart

It loves to dwell, and when the slow

And heavy hour is doom'd our part,

Its laughter on our grief will grow.

The minstrel ceas'd, and plaudits rung

From rock, and grove, and woody lair;

And morning's hymn from many a tongue

Did mingle with 't in midway air.

The minstrel ceas'd ; but deep in sleep

The maiden's lulled senses steep

And light before the fanning gale

The guideless vessel told the tale.

She rides the waves a lifeless thing,

With all of life's unflagged wing-

THE BRIDE OF LISMORE

A lily new pluckt from its stem,
Which neither death nor life can claim.
The soft winds lent their gentle aid
To reach the willow's weeping shade;
The vessel anchor'd in the creek,
Nor wist her heart that she was there;
Her elfin locks play'd on her cheek,
And eddied round her temples fair.

Wake! Helen, wake! the call of morn
From Achindain tower is sweetly borne!
Thy seat is empty in the hall,
An only child thou art, and all
A mother's fondness nurses thee.
Wake! Helen, wake! fear's in her e'e!
She wakes not yet. Again the peal
Of rising fear sweeps on the gale,
And, gathering round in panting grief,
Her maidens strive to yield relief,
And love untold 's now told in tears,
And gentle deeds in breathless fears.

THE BRIDE OF LISMORE

The maiden slept; but not the sleep
That nature yields the worn, I trow.
The maiden slept; but chill the weep
That gathers on her lily brow.
A heavy breast the waters bore;
The tear of grief is on the shore:
The minstrel's song had done its part;
For well she deem'd its sooth. Her heart
Cull'd in no hopes to sweeten grief,
Or gild with distant days' relief;
For long before the harper thrill'd
Of brighter days, her bosom chill'd
Beneath the load unconscious given
As tender flower et tempest riven.

   And long and deep the breath she drew,
Then sob on sob fast on her grew.
'Twas memory's rush - we seldom twice
Can look thereon, and dare it thrice.
Ere much of sleepless life arise
To prompt the sigh, and cloud the eyes,

THE BRIDE OF LISMORE

Full on her soul the sporting beam
Thrid lightnings flash, awoke the theme
Of what she felt, and feels - the pain
Reel'd madness through her aching brain.

By daisied walk and garden bower,
The rankling weed o'er tops the flower;
The violet breathes from lowly bed,
And blends their sweets ' neath careless tread;
The rose unfolds her swaddling bands,
Unprun'd, unpropp'd by gentle hands;
The frisking pet-lamb heedless strays,
And, wondering, bleats for by-gone days,
And licks the hand that used to stroke
This favour'd of the mountain flock:
But fails to gain a look, or trace
The prized boon-a smiling face.
But mortal breasts, though destin'd right
Amortal path, will catch respite:
And light will break, though clouds of dun
Veils thick o'er beams of cheering sun.

The Bride of Lismore.

PART SECOND.

> "'Tis true they are a lawless brood,
> But rough in form, nor mild in mood;
> And every creed, and every race,
> With them hath found-may find a place."
>
> — BYRON.

FAR to the west, a rock-girt isle,

Lies on the vast Atlantic's smile.

In distance viewed it seems a speck,

From far off isle, or rocking deck.

Then nigh'd two rocks together twines

Round channel'd waves, and reef-strew'd lines -

'Tis named by men the " Isle of Pines."

THE BRIDE OF LISMORE

One voice, one feeling swayed the isle -
One frown was all, and all one smile -
One spoke of death, and, all combin'd,
Was't mercy sway'd-alike they join'd.
One man, the captain of the crew
(For they were pirates, and not few
Their number), hinged on his breath
The law that yielded life or death.

They pirates on the eastern seas,
And westward hied as merchantmen;
In sooth, their freights of merchandise
Had ne'er belied the name. But then
The price of blood, of life, was theirs,
And all that life to man endears.
Full many a hope that skipp'd the wave
They'd plunged in a sullen grave;
Full many a tie that knit the heart
To friends and home, away, away,
Their stern command had doom'd to part,
And not a tongue was left to say.

THE BRIDE OF LISMORE

Wed to the waves, they felt not life,

Unless embroil'd in scenes of strife.

The lightnings sheen, the gulphing blast,

Spoke to their hearts as spoke the past.

The cutlass, sword, and arm of death,

Wrought round their hearts no pallid wreath;

And to no eye their eyes betray'd

Aught than hearts stern and undismay'd.

Such was their shadow. True, in such

Their days were whil'd by far too much;

But yet the sword that smote so keen,

And purple stream'd with deeds unseen,

Would sometimes pause, and wipe the blade,

And wend its way to others' aid.

Upon that night, when chafed waves

Roll'd o'er the dead, and ocean'd caves,

And careless play'd with bones, and gold,

And gems, and jewels, and toys untold,

Sea's heritage since days of old,

THE BRIDE OF LISMORE

The mermaid rose, and rode the waves,

Besprent with gems of ocean's caves;

And as she braided o'er her locks,

Loud rung her laugh through cavern'd rocks.

And, ever and anon, her tongue

A cadence wild to ocean sung.

That night saw Edwin's shallop tost,

And mortal eye said all but lost.

When to the Isle of Pines was bent

The pirate crew, and spied him spent,

And yielding to that fatal sleep,

Which over fainting bosoms creep,

They slacken sail, and quickly clasp

The unconscious prize from ocean's grasp;

Then brac'd the sails, and to the blast

The vessel creak'd o'er ocean's waste.

With cordage strained to other climes,

And scenes of unrepented crimes.

To-morrow's sun saw Edwin tost

On waves that lash'd the island coast,

THE BRIDE OF LISMORE

The rock-girt home of daring hearts,
Who bleed to brave what life imparts;
Nor felt his heart the shrinking pain
Of usage rude from ruthless men:
For deeds of blood, and deeds of love,
Upon their map were strangely wove.
Each strove to soothe, and such might won
Save thus to home, and lov'd ones gone.
And when his hope would withering fade,
And, drooping, hang her fainting head,
He sought the grove, and, silent, whil'd
His wayward griefs, where nature smil'd
In heedless splendour to this child,
And faintly hoped a day would come,
Would near him to his ocean'd home,
And those he lov'd: The captain's voice
Claimed him his own, and bade rejoice
Each buoyant heart, and welcome sound,
To sooth his spirit's latent wound.

THE BRIDE OF LISMORE

And often by the wave-worn beach
His footsteps bent, and eye would stretch,
Till ocean melted into sky,
And, guideless, strain'd the weary eye.

Then he would solace seek from thought,
And fathom deep where phantoms wrought.
Mayhap this wave, whose frothy crest
Skims wildly over ocean's breast,
Has swept the coast, and heard the tale
Of maiden's grief, and mother's wail;
Or wilder thoughts would him assail -
Mayhap she sleeps in ocean's bed,
Or daring hands her bosom's bled;
Then would he start, and, shuddering, clasp.
(For parted hearts will shadows grasp,
Or aught the heart can beg or buy,
The rankling wound to mollify.)
Until stern life call'd him to join
The joys that lack'd the heart's entwine;

THE BRIDE OF LISMORE

Or woo'd the hour when day would close,

To sink his eyes in night's repose.

Alas! no rose blooms for the heart

That met, and lov'd, and bled to part -

No dewy morn, no shady eve,

Nor noon-day beauties can deceive;

Nor life, with all its dazzling sheen,

Can all undo what once has been.

And there shone damsels in the isle,

That might a stranger's heart beguile;

Though swarthy-featur'd, yet their eyes

Soft tinkled tales youth can't despise.

But she, the beauty of the isle,

Was fairer far, and shone her smile

As Peri eyes in midnight dream,

Or moonbeams on the glittering stream.

When from a cloud of deepening blue

(Of skies and eyes the loveliest hue),

Her brightening beams fall on the water,

So sweetly shone this island daughter.

THE BRIDE OF LISMORE

Her curled locks in gems arrayed,

And much of worth lay on her breast;

You would not deem'd that she had stray'd

In vulgar throng, though meanly drest .

And there was much of lady love

That witching wrought her smiles' subdue.

That when the tongue in speech would rove,

The silver sound found nought to do.

There rode a majesty of air,

A self-possession of her all,

And on her brow there sate no care

Bespoke her portion mixed with gall.

The Corsair's only daughter she,

And all that knit his years to joy?

A Saxon dame was doom'd to be

The mother of this maid. A boy

Twin'd with her, but his infant bloom

Lies blasted in the hallowed tomb,

A small niche in the cocoa grove.

The fragrant myrtle, jessamine,

THE BRIDE OF LISMORE

With roses in the web is wove,
That marks the peaceful spot. At e'en
The humming bird his plumage fair
Decks on a rosebud, sips the dew,
Lies globul'd in the blushing lair,
And briefly hymns the day's adieu.

I love these spots. What, though there's none
To say who owns each crumbling bone?
What, though no human tongue does bear
The chime of life upon your ear?
Though silence wakes not to your tread,
And echo slumbers with the dead?
Yet the appalling silence wind
A pleasing shadow o'er the mind;
And from the turf where daisies bloom,
And lank grass wantons o'er the tomb,
A truth's reveal'd to breathing dust,
Engrav'd on lines, where cankering rust
Gainsays each hope of mortal trust.

THE BRIDE OF LISMORE

And I have said no cares her prest,

Yet would another's barb her breast;

Her father's feats she often mourn'd

In soft remonstrance of the child,

And to her pleading eye has turn'd

The fiat dark-omened features piled:

For she was all, as has been sung,

Whereon his lamp of years was hung,

And father's heart round such will twine

More than can tongue or pen define.

And Edwin pants for lands beneath

A cooler sky, where's hill and heath,

And rocky glens, and freedom's sons -

A land where rest his father's bones,

Where ties unloos'd, and legends wrote,

Lie wrapt in soul - mysterious thought!

Whose bud expands amid the waste

Of breakers wild in mortal breast,

And bids us live, though adverse skies

We, wondering, grope where hope would rise.

THE BRIDE OF LISMORE

The wish is vain - yet such will spring

In bosoms buoy'd on wisdom's wing,

And some sweet spot lives in the breast

The exile claims his home of rest,

Where willows weep, and yew-tree waves

Its shadow o'er the home of graves.

Here boyhood whil'd his thoughtless time,

Nor dar'd to dream of other clime;

Nor yet life's secrets on his brow,

And yet his cares and fears were few;

And weeps, and fondly hopes, when, tempests past,

And brighter skies have dawn'd at last,

A pledge redeem'd, some brother's hand

Will bear him to his father's land,

And press once more its peebly strand,

Though dust to dust, and such has given

To parting life a ray of heaven,

And blended into bliss sublime

Of joyful song's last sighs of time.

THE BRIDE OF LISMORE

The captain frown'd as Edwin dar'd

To name the land his bosom shar'd,

Yet deigned to smile, presaging good,

Well known to men that mark'd his mood.

Alas! his heart was taught betimes

That tinsell'd life is painted crimes.

His mother's home and cabin stood

Where rolls the Tiber's rapid flood -

A widow'd home. She loved her son,

And mother's love more warmly run,

'Cause he was all. One day to spend

With distant friend her steps did wend.

A stranger call'd, and luring smil'd,

And from a mother's home was wil'd

This youth of years, and on the sea

First sip'd the draught of treachery.

Sore bent with labour, long opprest

With thoughts of home, and joys unblest,

He rose at last by powerful hand

And daring heart to wield command;

THE BRIDE OF LISMORE

But long ere this, to morning years
Of infant joys, and mother's cares
His heart was bronzed o'er, and thought
Scarce wing'd to days almost forgot.

"My mountain home and mother dear,"
Sigh'd Edwin on the captain's ear.
The Tiber's wave - the orange bloom -
A mother's cabin - infant home
Flash'd o'er the mind a magic spell;
For nature limns her pictures well:
He turn'd and hid his quivering face,
And speech essay'd in soften'd grace:
" You have a mother - go in peace."

Again to sea - to sea's the word -
And action nerves the slacken'd cord,
Beats high each breast, and o'er the wave
They seek and find a prize or − grave -

THE BRIDE OF LISMORE

A something rude to break the crust

That gathers round ambitious dust -

Which flickering wastes 'midst pausing days,

On deeds unworthy blame or praise.

And eastward bore, through waves and tides,

Of breeze and calm, the vessel glides,

And breakers nigh - a rugged shore,

Yet dear to one, the vessel bore.

Our native land! No freshening breeze

E'er stole the balm from flower or trees

To nerve the stream that lags behind,

The rosy cheek, and cheerful mind,

Are half so sweet as sight of thee!

When straining o'er the deep blue sea,

Sight rests upon the summit's wild,

Where parting day's last glories smil'd,

Some rock, or tree, or antique tower,

That us'd to greet our natal hour,

THE BRIDE OF LISMORE

Breaks on the view, and pilots on

The train of thought to days a-gone.

Do roses bloom, and linnets chaunt,

As sweet and fair as they were wont?

Lives in yon halls, where infant sight

First broke on beams of cheering light,

One throbbing breast, where garner'd lies

The heart's untold, hope's unreap'd, prize?

Again the chime of Edwin's voice

Sounds in his halls, and bids rejoice

A mother's heart, nor her alone,

The halo gilds o'er every one.

And service, bent 'neath tottering years,

Claims right to mingle joyful tears,

And youthful cheeks; and frisking bound

The watch-dog to the well-known sound.

More sweet the roses breathe - the thrush

Yields sweeter notes from hawthorn bush,

THE BRIDE OF LISMORE

And gladness wakes in melting strain
Through all of nature's wide domain.
When long lost hearts return again,
Have ye not felt and learn'd to prize
The silent joys, the throbbing sighs
That burst to life in breathless haste?
When hearts commingle, hands are prest,
Innur'd to brook what absence knows,
And griefs untold hearts can't disclose.

And spring and summer wept and smil'd
'Neath sun and shower, and winter wild
Had sung to rest as wayward child,
And vital breath to plant and flower
Breath'd fragrance o'er the spring-tide hour.
The thrush, the cuckoo's note, again
Swept down the vale in gladden'd strain,
And hearts beat light in Lismore's isle,
As they were wont at nature's smile,

THE BRIDE OF LISMORE

As they were wont! The grove and bower,

The ocean'd shore at sunset hour,

The pathless path, could such express

The haunts of pensive loneliness!

For hearts o'ercast will scarcely deign

To link with things of mortal ken -

Would echo sighs, and woo relief

From days of bliss unknown to grief.

And some such tale as this would rise

At twilight's hour, on memory's sighs;

Whilst wreathed round a feathery cloud,

That poises o'er the evening's smile,

Is the blushing fringe, the morning's woo'd

To some far-circling ocean'd isle.

" O, dawn ye on the land of bliss?

Or dawn ye on the brows of care?

Does morning reap the evening's wish?

Or breathes it on - my spirit, where?

O! think not, say not fruitless prayer!

THE BRIDE OF LISMORE

O, wreathes of joy my temples bind,

For they are heavy. There was a voice;

Could I amongst the living find

That voice, I would again rejoice.

But that is past, and I am sad;

The wise will sigh and pity me;

My hopes unhing'd will fools be glad; -

Oh no! 'twere cruel-it cannot be.

There was a time my listless breast

Deem'd life not so, but pilgrim peace

Has drawn my groves, and strew'd a waste

Of trackless gloom each sigh increase.

There was a time, when I could brace

The sighs of life in reason's keeping,

And gather tears to silent pace

The bed of death - the couch of weeping.

But now my sorrow's all my own,

I gather tears from silent thinking,

And sighs spring up where there has grown

A tender plant, from life I'm shrinking -

THE BRIDE OF LISMORE

From death I wander not - the gloom
He spreads round hearts that foster years,
Would light my taper to the tomb,
And shroud the woes my nature wears."

One morn to morning's pleasure share
She wander'd o'er the peebly beach,
And there was in her face and air
More than the past had deign'd to teach.
She look'd upon the rocking wave;
She farther look'd on yonder shore;
And mildly shone the look she gave,
As if it breathed - " I weep no more. "
Yet festering grief will lurking grow
Around the heart, and prove the foe
Of reason ; - e'en where reason long
Has deem'd that mourning forms a wrong.

And nature woos, and won repose:
She leant her where the daisy grows;

THE BRIDE OF LISMORE

The tufting violet bore her head,

And breath'd its fragrance o'er the maid.

She wanders o'er the vision'd past,

And oft was breath'd in softest sound

A name that all the wintry waste

Had not effac'd - 'twas memory bound -

In ecstacies of all her breast

Deem'd as the balm of her despair,

Her willing arms were wildly prest

Around the void of subtle air.

A voice was spoke: a sudden heave

Bade fade the scenes she dearly priz'd:

Her eyes she op'd, nor op'd to grieve

Her vision-all is realis'd.

And the joy that's bled for, the sweetest, the best,

Its halo shall shed o'er the hopes of his breast.

To a Friend, Barca, India.

To climes of the east, where the bright beaming ray

Darts curtainless forth on the sickening day,

Where the Ganges' proud bears on its trade-studded breast,

The trophies which nation to nation bequest.

To the gray walls of Dacca, where busily plies

The fingers which cunning so artful devise,

O'er the rich braided fabric, yet destin'd to won

On the fair sylphs of Britain, or palac'd saloon,

My gratitude's tender'd, accept it, ye good,

Yet remembering " the land of the mountain and flood;"

For Dacca's best treasures to me and to mine,

A heart there beats for me, for days of " langsyne."

Do you think of the glen, of the hill, or the tower,

Of the Lunan's soft murmurs through hazelly bower,

Where infancy whiled a brief sunny hour?

TO A FRIEND, BACCA, INDIA

Of the faces that melted in life's happiness?
Of the hearts that could yield the endearing caress?
The hill, and the glen, and the gray nodding tower,
And the riv'let's soft murmurs through canopied bower,
Seem the same as they were in your boyhood's hour;
But the faces that smil'd, and the hearts that carest,
When your footsteps first came from the isles of the east,
Have long slumbered in silence, with scarcely a speck
To say where is stranded mortality's wreck.
A niche in the chancel - the house of our God,
Yet retains a lov'd name in the sacred abode.
And we weep as we ponder o'er things that are not,
That soon this last relic will too be forgot;
But there is a record - a page that retains,
Though time stamps his foot on our crumbling remains:
May our names be there wrote, and those that are dear,
When the swellings of Jordan will break on our ear.

NOTE

ON

LINES TO A FRIEND, DACCA.

THAT friend I first met in the person of a fair-haired boy, of five or six years of age, nearly thirty years ago. He came from the isle of France, of which he is a native, to a friend in this locality, and was so far entrusted to my care in school-boy days; but that friend with whom he resided fell asleep, the sleep of mortality, and the fair-haired boy left me, destined a stranger in a strange land. I lost sight of him until last year, when a kind communication from his hand reached me. Such communication suggested my lines. The hill and castle of Guthrie, with the glen of the district, the Lunan murmuring through the meadows, the niche in the chancel being the marble monument in the church, will recall, to him at least, the dreams of early days.

Adrian,

TO HIS SOUL, WHEN DYING.

Ah! now my soul! thou fleeting thing,
Thou dear companion of this breast,
Say whether spreads thy trembling wing?
Where is the region of thy rest?
Thou pleasing thing! where is thy mirth?
Why is thy gaiety turn'd to sighing?
Thus verging from the realms of earth,
My soul, ah! whither art thou flying?

The Blind Man's Dog.

'NEATH yonder turf that draws no eye
By sculptor's art or flattery,
The blind man sleeps. Long known and seen
To pace the round where's youth had been.
To pace! With whom? My pen misgives.
Ono! his guide yet o'er him lives.
Laid on the turf, his heavy heart
Ill brooks that life from life should part.
The evening soothes him with the morrow,
But morning comes, and still in sorrow;
And if he sleeps, 'tis not the sleep
That us'd to yield his heart repose.
The night winds o'er him pallid creep;
He starts, and deems the rustling foes.

A BLIND MANS DOG

Anon their music guiles his ear,

As all his heart heav'd for, and heaves;

And oft the fruitless pause to hear

Lies on his breath, the yellow leaves

Fall eddying in the gathering gloom,

Yet still he clings unto the tomb.

Alas! for him's no home, no voice,

In tones well known, bids him rejoice;

No guidless hand to pat his head,

And portion out his sweet brown bread.

This could not last. Both sleeps the sleep

That wakes not here to pine and weep.

No bosom heaves - no tear is shed

Above their lone and lowly bed.

Lines to a Linnet.

[In a severe winter, a linnet was caught which I nursed until the return of spring; then returned it to its native bowers. Such suggested the following lines: -]

Now, when the silver'd voice of spring
Has sung the angry north to rest,
And zephyrs on their downy wing
Cull fragrance from the violet's breast.
When in the shade the cowslips peep,
Primroses court the sunny height,
And nature, rousing from her sleep,
Shakes off the hoary weeds of night
When from the grove is borne a voice
Makes man to blush a conscious shame, -
Ye little songster, there rejoice,
Make gratitude alike your theme;

LINES TO A LINNET

And say, thou little songster, say

That thou wilt cheer my lonely rove,

When balmy May lures me to stray

Down through the furze, or fragrant grove;

Or, seated on the daisy sward,

I sip the sweets of life serene,

Enhale the breeze with fond regard,

That nerves anew my lagging vein,

There, hymning to the blooming year,

Or cheering her who lonely sits

In yonder furze, or blossom'd briar,

And fondly lists your soothing sweets.

At sight of me thy narrow bounds,

Thy seed-box, stor'd to linnet's taste,

You'll think of these, and nature's frowns,

And, grateful, swell your little breast.

Little songster! fare-thee-well!

May summer's sweets be sweetly thine!

And may you find in winter's swell

Abreast replete with love as mine!

May urchin hands ne'er find the bough

LINES TO A LINNET

That friendly shades thy little all!

Nor e'er, to please thy natal glow,

Be taught to mourn thy freedom's fall!

Should hearts the woodland songster meet

Would stem with death its vocal powers,

O, think! it is a linnet sweet

That sweet would cheer your lingering hours!

A Fragment on Marco Bozzari,

THE MODERN GREEK PATRIOT.

"Greece, thine ancient lamp is spent;
Thou art thine own monument;
But the sepulchre is rent,
And a wind is on the wing,
At whose breath new heroes spring,
Sages teach, and poets sing."
MONTGOMERY.

"For freedom's battle once begun,
Bequeath'd by bleeding sire to son,
Though baffled oft, is ever won."
BYRON.

THE daring exploit which he achieved the night on which he fell, August 20, 1823, was worthy Greece in her better days. With his small but faithful band of Suliotes, he was lying in wait to intercept the chief of Scutari, who was advancing with his turbaned host, and reckoning on victory.

Bozzari, stung to the heart for his country's wrongs, formed the resolution of penetrating their camp in the silence of midnight, as he had learned the Turkish watchword. At the head of his band he told his mind, but added, I will be followed by none but volunteers - volunteers

A FRAGMENT ON MARCO ROZZARI

for their country! Every one thirsted for Turkish blood, and one voice proclaimed them all volunteers. The fact is as related: he was wounded, and stooping on his knee to reload, a fatal shot laid him low. His followers burst through, and bore his body with them.

He rose, and, stooping on his knee,
The patriot nerv'd his ebbing breast,
He aim'd his tube, " This for the free!"
He said, and fired, with death- borne haste.
The turbans roll, and houris sung
The requiem hymn with syren tongue;
The turbans roll, but he was smote-
He breath'd not, eyed not earth again;
And death with death was dearly bought,
Bozzari pil'd the piled slain.
Then rose the yell, the Othman cry, -
"Mahomet − Allah - victory! "
Eve clos'd on ranks in silence hush'd,
The midnight heard the clang of strife,
The morning broke, but morning blush'd,
For all it could not wake to life.

A FRAGMENT ON MARCO ROZZARI

And Suliote, Othman, mix'd their blood,

And kiss'd the turf so proudly trod,

And horse and rider, in one mass,

Lay stiff, and cold, on clotted grass.

And through the densed breath of war,

Flash'd ataghan, or seymitar;

Though splinter'd still, the hilt, untied,

That told where maddening strife had died.

And if there was a pulse unrun,

'Twas ebbing fast; long ere were spun

The spiry shadows of the eve,

That feeble pulse had ceas'd to heave.

A turban'd host on Grecian ground!

Away, away, it cannot be!

Rise, heroes! strike the martial sound -

Greece only blooms to nurse the free -

A turban'd host on Grecian ground!

My country blush - she looks to thee.

Make freedom yet for her resound,

Her passed glories all to be.

NOTE

ON

FRAGMENT TO MARCO BOZZARI.

LAND of renowned shades! lives there a heart who heaves not a sigh for thy fallen, and freedom-stinted shores? and now, when the balance is poising in the hand of Fate, who breathes not a prayer for thee, the land that first dawned on the name of Christian, in whose archives was first wrote their names who dared to die to maintain its glorious cause? That the Sun of thy morning would break the despotic gloom that has be-nighted thee; that the hand of freedom would be stretched to raise a fallen sister, nay, rather mother. Hail Greece as the mother of the sciences we inherit!

On Seeing Lord Byron's Birth in the British Peerage.

From hence we date what all are proud to show,
The glittering trappings of a titled birth;
And hence we date, too, what's unbid to blow -
Our Upas-bloom - the gifts of parent earth.
But who shall date, or mark the subtile grow
Of souls as his, whom genius, in her mirth,
Has dower'd with fancy, fire to all express
We've felt, or feel, its worth, or nothingness.

Mutual Love.

There is a sigh that speaks to mine
The tender tale of mutual love:
There is a heart I cannot tine,
With mine it is so closely wove:
There is an eye I love to meet,
It speaks of peace, nor harbours dread:
There is a breast, and O! 'tis sweet
To pillow on't my weary head:
There is a voice that wins my soul
More than the music-breathing lyre:
There is a face, whose soft control
Sheds brightness o'er my brows of care:
There is a form, a soul I love,
O! could I live, and love it less!
Ye gods forbid! love's from above -
O! shower it 'yond my faint express.

The Author's Father. -1829.

HE yet survives. Long may he share
The sweets of life, my ardent prayer.
Though like a tree where forests grew,
The axe has levelled all but few.
That few how hard to congregate?
Of silent beds, homes desolate!
How many, that life's morning sun
Stream'd on their race of life begun!
His bosom friend long sleeps in dust,
And they who form'd his earthly trust.
But yet, though nature feebly wears,
And sometimes seeks relief in tears,
He knows of whom that truth's reveal'd -
"Thou art my God, my Sun, and Shield!"
And, leaning on that rock, surveys
A dear Redeemer's purchas'd prize.

THE AUTHOR'S FATHER - NOTE

A hand, though wreath'd in mystery here,

Will kindly wipe the falling tear,

And gather, when time's race is run,

A family round their Father's throne.

NOTE.

My mother died in 1807, and disease carried off my two eldest brothers in 1810.

To the Robin.

THE honeysuckle rising 'midst a wreath
Of falling blossoms of the fading rose?
A note vibrates from yonder bending boughs
That canopies o'er Lunan's placid stream.
These notes at dawn, and closing day, convey
To Scotia's sons and groves a well-known strain, -
A strain that cheers the young years' budding scene -
That mellow-mourns her sear and falling leaves;
And, from the hoary spray, how sweetly flows,
When wintry blasts their ruthless fetters clank,
Oh! truce the youthful hand, and bear not hence
To wring a parent's heart their fledging care,
Nor fatal dart the blood-fraught aimed stone
To deeper tinge his rosy trusting breast.
Ah! little think your hearts whilst thus they bound,
And o'er the death - calm'd wing exulting heave,
You've broken nature's sweet and hallow'd ties -
Have sent a widow'd mourner through the grove.

Innate Philosophy.

DISLIMN my fancy of that shaded ground,
And mantling grief would tard each brighter hour;
Dispel the gloom with which my muse is bound,
And I should ask where is her pleasing power.
Man's life's a flickering reed; yet there is o'er
His chequer'd map a spell that stubborn lives:
It stamps him in the sunny sky, the shower,
The virent cheek, the bay of life it heaves,
And, nor in death, it labours faintest to deceive's.
Such is that innate bent the free- will growth,
We can't dissemble, though 'twere doubly wise.
Delusion's charm! a plaything of our youth,
With which we journied on, and begg'd supplies -
Unconscious begg'd our after smiles or sighs.
And why? In giddy years our helm is whet,
As if an after year would not suffice.
In that, at least, we show we'd discomfit
Life's run, and value time, as time to us is let.

Recollections

BROKE on my youth, and shone on me,

A lovely star: I'd fondly be

In youth again to call it mine;

For such it was, for me did shine.

For what of life I'd quaff'd, there still

Was thirst upon my tongue, until

Its radiance beam'd ; then such would cease ;

It seem'd my spirit's resting place,

Bloom of my life unconsciously;

For life partook her beauty's dye,

And I had deemed her beautiful

'Yond aught this world had lent my will.

We lov'd, and parted; 'twere unwise

To while our days 'twixt heart and eyes;

For on the stage we'd newly trod,

Life dower'd our love a wide abode.

RECOLLECTIONS

We parted! Parting had not been

More sad, when life and death between,

The midnight spoke the hour, the sky

Hung out no light-the night winds sigh -

And o'er us sadly heaved a yew,

(For by the dead we breath'd adieu).

I cannot paint, nor yet express,

What then was felt: such conflicts lie

Beyond the reckless, shallow guess,

Or gazings of a listless eye,

That hour of sadness long gone bye,

Speaks to my heart what cannot die.

Years fled, and seasons smil'd and frown'd.

Again we met - again we own'd

A love, confess'd before we spoke;

For o'er her face a hectic broke,

And told my heart in secrecy

A pulse beat true to love and me.

I know no more. A darkening cloud

Fell on my brain-wrapp'd in the shroud

RECOLLECTIONS

My spirit warr'd with life and clay -
And long'd to meet a purer day.
I know no more. My last of life
Had well nigh perish'd in the strife;
But youth sustain'd, and years to run
Broke forth anew my clouded sun;
And life broke forth, and memory came,
And with it ties I longed to claim.
My eyes were dim, so well nigh seal'd
On all I knew that life reveal'd.
But well I mark'd who watch'd the stream
Of life run deeper, conn'd each name
They all unlike.
And when I ask'd where she was gone,
" She's laid by yonder added stone,"
Was answer'd, with a look of woe,
My heart grew chill!

Within my breast once beat a pulse,
And all for one, and no one else.

RECOLLECTIONS

That one is gone, and in her grave;

My heart bled sore, but could not save;

And o'er that pulse a thought will stray,

That wings me to another day.

'Tis sorrow born in silence nurst?

Remnant of love that sway'd me first?

I cannot quit, nor yet possess.

Sting to the breast, it cannot bless

A seared leaf-a bud of care?

Remembrancer that such things were!

On the Snow - Drop.

SWEET floweret! pledge of coming spring,

Through nature's frowns thou rear'st thy head,

Whilst to thy spotless breast do cling

The chilly snows, with hoar pourtray'd.

Sure, lovely flower, yet cold's thy bed,

And cold the shelter thou dost share;

Yet lonely thou, by nature's aid,

Awak'st to hail the infant year.

Ere yet the minstrel lark does pour

His morning salutations forth, -

Ere yet the thrush, from nature's bower,

The eventide salutes with mirth, -

Yet thou glint'st forth, in humble birth,

Presuming, yet in guileless guise;

But soon, alas! to parent earth

The ruthless blasts resign their prize.

ON THE SNOW-DROP

Short are thy days, and fair thy form,

Thou emblem of the blushing fair,

Like thee they bud beneath the storm -

Like thee, they bloom in shelters bare.

Whilst flattery weaves a silken snare

To keener sting fond hopes betray'd,

Then howling blasts with heedless stare,

Lay low the snow-drop and the maid.

Paul before Agrippa,

Acts, Chap. xxvi., Verse 28-29.

"To be a
Christian, Paul, thou almost me persuad'st. "
Almost! The champion of the Christian faith
Glanc'd at the partial sound-he ey'd the scene:
The eagle-blazon'd dome, the fulgent throne,
The eager gaze of Roman senators,
And martial band,s that wait on regal pomp,
Serv'd these to awe his soul to servile means?
Or languish'd he beneath his chains, to grasp
Their wealth, or boasted power emboss'd in guilt?
Ah, no! As water cheers the languid herb,
So heavenly comfort swell'd his placid soul;
He breath'd benevolence o'er the guilty throng,
And thus replied, nor fear'd wrath's tumult ought -

PAUL BEFORE AGRIPPA.

" I would to God that thou, O king! and all
That hear my voice this day, were not almost,
But altogether, such as I, except these bonds. "
Ah then! my soul, shrink not, but nobly dare
To grasp thy faith, though persecutions roar;
Or sophistry, in milder form, may thwart
Her poison'd chalice o'er thy guardless hour.
Ah! shrink not - Paul these overcame, and he
Was only feeble man, yet fraught with grace.
Nor was it from the learned Gamaliel
He conn'd this lesson - no, 'twas Heaven itself
He crav'd repentant, whilst contrition's tears
Lav'd smooth the sand his persecuting arm
Had error - heap'd, and stained with hostile gore.
This he, who, passing unto greater trials,
Did from Miletus to Ephesus send
(Once mighty city, when the Roman reins,
Uncurbed, flowed on Asia's fertile shores -
Now prostrate all its splendour in the dust,
And wafted as the spray of ages gone),

PAUL BEFORE AGRIPPA.

And call'd the elders of its infant church
He erst had planted - to them boldly showed
How he had preached that Christ was all
To him and them, and for the prize to fight,
Though blood and death stood 'twixt them and the
    crown.

From Scenes of Palestine.

MARK, Chap. x.

"The hundred-gated cities then,
The towers and temples, nam'd of men
Eternal, and the thrones of kings;
The gilded summer palaces;
The courtly bowers of love and ease,
Where still the bird of pleasure sings
Ask ye the destiny of them?
Go, gaze on fallen Jerusalem!
                    MILMAN.

THE waters of Jordan roll on to the sea,

Through wilderness windings, to blue Galilee,

Diffusing her riches through valley and hill,

Where industry smiles, or flocks wander at will.

The vintage hangs mellow, and gladdening the smile

Of the valley's reward for the husbandman's toil;

The olive-bough bends, and drops from the tree,

And crags of the wilderness sweets of the bee,

FROM SCENES OF PALESTINE.

And sweetly the song from upland and vale,

Which the daughters of Judah soft waft on the gale;

Perhaps 'tis an air which plaintive recall

The sighs of their fathers - their nation's downfall,

When captive they lay by proud Babylon,

And, pondering, weep'd for their favoured Zion;

Or the air may be lighter, unveiling the gloom,

When the desert as Carmel and Sharon will bloom,

And the ransom'd of Israel will join in the hymn,

That awaits the redeem'd of nation and clime;

But Judah, though blooming, breath'd sorrows and pain -

The sorrows which waylay the children of men.

The strength of the mighty, and beauty's bright bust,

Are nearly allied to the frail things of dust.

Bartimeus, the poor and despis'd of her sons,

Long'd to share in the blessings of more favour'd ones.

Ah! helpless he sat by the wayside to plead

With the thoughtless and vain for the blessings of bread.

With the thoughtless and vain! O, is it not true

That the helpless of mankind have much to subdue?

FROM SCENES OF PALESTINE.

To bury in silence the proud one's rebuke,

And submit, with a smile, to the pain-giving look!

And he sat by the wayside, the cool fanning breeze

Swept over the vineyards and lofty palm trees,

With their balmy-knit treasures, sweet soothers of pain;

But fairest of bloosoms bloomed for him in vain.

The Galilean passed - O passed he as one

Esteemed and caressed by the children of men?

Or heard he the pleading, and passed in haste,

With the gaze of the Levite, or gait of the priest?

The Galilean passed-but he passed not as one

Esteemed and caressed by the children of men;

No beauty or comeliness beam'd from his brow -

Despis'd and rejected by all but a few,

And the hour of peril too fatally prov'd

That self is esteem'd 'yond all that's belov'd.

The Galilean passed - but he passed not in haste,

For the tender of mercy was dear to his breast;

Yea, dear to his soul, for his errand was love,

Proclaimed unto man from the mansions above.

FROM SCENES FROM PALESTINE.

He ask'd his petition - O! what were more kind

Than the sweet streaming light to the eyes of the blind?

'Twas a long- cherish'd wish - a hope that illum'd

The spirit's dark wanderings thus living entomb'd.

He ask'd his petition: " Oh! give me to see

The land of my birth-the lofty palm tree -

The mountains of Judah, my fathers have trod -

The city of Zion, our God's lov'd abode! "

The petition is granted - his faith is approv'd -

He look'd on the beauties his vision had lov'd;

And gratitude warm'd, and boundless to one -

That one the despis'd, yet belov'd Galilean.

To Memory.

> "His mother's cabin-home that lay
> Where feathery cocoas fringe the bay;
> The dashing of his brethren's oar;
> The conch-note heard along the shore,
> All through his wakening bosom swept:
> He clasp'd his country's Tree, and wept!"
> HEMANS.

I.

ON days of early morn will eager fix

The heart with melting pleasure, and again

O'er travel stamping scenes imparting mix

Of what we have been, and may be; and then

Arising soothing dream will swathe the brain;

And all but footsteps on the dewy lawn

Will greet our view, and blend each loved scene

With gildings of the past, where first the dawn

Of life was shed; nor though we're fled, is all withdrawn.

TO MEMORY.

II.

And such some well known tune of treasur'd days,

When infant home and joys were warmly knit,

Recalls to life, though on our brow the bays

Of years unfold a blossom verging into night,

And through the vista winding glance the might

Is felt, and breath'd in sighs hearts can't suppress;

And tears will mingle o'er the loved sight,

More than the reckless breast could dream or guess,

Far less my feeble pen could all such thoughts express.

III.

Some idle page as this a face recalls,

Where features play'd that sweeten'd hours of time;

Some moss-clad stone by yonder ivied walls

Decyphers names of annal'd worth or crime;

But such memorials fade: the syren hymn

That pleas'd in youth, to chasten'd life redeems

But shadows of the past, whereon will chime

Achord coinciding, where thought silent teems

With all we priz'd of life - revealed as passed dreams.

TO MEMORY.

IV.

And such memorials fade: the musty page
Fast crumbles into dust; the mossy stone
Forgets to show the sculptor's art, or wage
With time a lengthen'd war, what we have won
From mysteries of the past, all, all roll on
To shoreless tides, stamp'd with the wise decree
Man's gainsays can't revoke, nor yet atone
For blighted blossoms on the fruitless tree
Of wasted life, fast sweeping to eternity.

V.

Yet man will trophies raise, and eager grasp
The column'd niche, whereon to 'grave a name;
And from the future, oh! how fondly clasp
At sweets, as if the niggard present were to blame.
But grasping minds oft graspless fabrics claim,
Whereon to blazon names; a poet's flickering lay,
That briefly blossoms into being, a theme
Ignites the living mass for one short day
Of breathless turmoil, whilst the sparkling bubbles play.

TO MEMORY.

VI.

And trouble springs from such, and something more

Than dates a being from this mortal round

Will fret the soul, and from the inmost core

Ooze bitter sorrows from the festering wound.

And why? From such polluted founts abound

A slime corrosive to man's nobler end,

For which his spirit dawn'd on earth, a sound

Of many tongues, engrossing all, where bend

The heart and knee at shrines true wisdom never ken'd.

VII.

And such is idol worship, crafty taught

From hearts beneath the guise of seeking fame.

The Indian pauses o'er our deeds, and straight

Condemns the tongue that echos not our shame.

And who shall say that he has dar'd to blame

Beyond the pale of truth? The Banian shade

Veils o'er his offerings to the hallowed name

He fears. We kneel to idols we have made,

And dare forget the hand that gives our daily bread.

TO MEMORY.

VIII.

But I digress. Why is yon mother's face
Suffused with grief, where sorrows, sadly coil'd,
Have stamp'd with wither'd age each youthful trace?
Some fair-haired boy flits by, whose visage mild
Recalls the features of a once lov'd child.
Oh! say not once, such faint conveys the joy
And age of mother's love, where nature thrill'd,
Or else her eye has caught some book, or toy,
Or dress, that us'd to please her own fair-haired boy.

IX.

And he sleeps in the dust, but dear the sod
That wraps his little breast. The careless foot
Of stranger, wending to the house of God,
Gives to her heart a knell. Deep silent thought
Oft bears her to the dear and hallow'd spot,
Where converse with the dust assuages pain;
And oft her heart would almost chide the lot
That made her childless, till some loved one
Points to the Christian page - "Thy son shall live again."

TO MEMORY.

X,

Yes, he shall live, though never more to claim

Th' unwearied vigils of a mother's care,

Or breathe his little joys beneath the beam

Which hope had pedestall'd on fondest prayer;

Or weave a garland from the flowerets fair

That deck the mead, or hawthorn's snowy breast:

All these are still'd. A treasur'd lock of hair

She oft-times ponders o'er with anxious haste,

As if the world would grudge what yields her bosom rest.

XI.

Ay, it will grudge, and chide with apathy

Each prize affliction severs from its own,

And, struggling for its victim, sound the cry

Of peace, when he who wounded says there's none.

So spake Judea, when her glittering crown,

Awing many nations, trembling, kiss'd the dust.

So speaks the world, and hastes to trample down

The feeble spark, the half-form'd wish, whose trust

Would centre on the arm who gave the fatal thrust.

TO MEMORY.

XII.

And he shall live - strange thought! - when all expire
Man claims a kindred too from knowledge streams,
Or secrets hid, that yet may waste their fire
On generations yet to come. The beams
Of sun and moon shall cease, and twinkling gleams
Of lesser orbs, when he whose high behest
Brought them and us to being, to join in themes
Faint breath'd in time, shall call them all to rest.
Man's spirit dares to live a doom'd or favour'd guest.

XIII.

And there are thoughts which language fails to bring
Beyond the confines of the beating breast,
And thoughts that flutter as the captive wing
Of eagle, struggling for his aerial nest;
And such the midnight hour awards, when rest
Renews the pilgrim of life's weary toil.
The hand that sleeps in dust is warmly prest,
And well-known features smile - the winning smile
Oft taught us of a peace, and joy, unmix'd with guile.

TO MEMORY.

XIV.

A farewell breath'd from quivering lips conveys

The dear remembrance of some sunny spot,

Where valu'd friendship knit the subtile ties,

Now only blooming from deep cherished thought.

Such is the breaking up of life, oft wrote

In legends deepest where we fondest lean;

The guide of youth, and those who would have fought

For feeble age the fight years can't sustain,

And who would patronis'd such feeble verse as mine.

XV.

Such fans the heart - sweet as the virgin fan

Of morn, untainted by the slime of day,

Fans on the aching brow. There is in man

What he will ponder o'er, yet blush to say,

A timid weak makes merit almost play

A worthless part, and in the dusky shade

Of dark oblivion hew a tomb, and lay

The price of future fame, untimely paid,

Which only springs to life, when all of man's decay'd.

TO MEMORY.

XVI.

But who is there that writes as he would wish,
Or deems his pen could speak his every thought?
E'en vigour's burstings into shadows rush
Of what the soul conceiv'd, and man has not
Wherewith to bring to life the birth he sought;
And such the spirit's warfare with the dust,
A breathing after more than man has got
Wherewith to shield a name from moth and rust
Of changeful life: so frail is all of mortal trust.

XVII.

In my land's lineage, be it mine to live,
Though only treasur'd in the hearts of few:
And be that few of those who dare to give
The meed of praise, or blame, where justly due.
Mayhap some pondering breast may yet rescue
Some features dear from memory's slippery page,
And bubbling founts, where joy and sorrows threw
Their varied streams around the heritage
Which time had portioned mine, life's weary pilgrimage.

The End

A BRIEF HISTORY
OF THE HERALD FAMILY
IN SCOTLAND

The Herald Family Name in Scotland
Statistics 1555 - 1850

The surname Herald was first noted in Argyllshire, the region of western Scotland corresponding roughly with the ancient Kingdom of Dál Riata, in the Strathclyde region of Scotland. The name appears several times in the Doomsday book, as there were several Herald families in England and Wales in 1086. There are several variants of the name including Herauld, Hearld, Harold, Harald and Heralt.

By the 1550s, Scottish families with the name of Herald[1] were very much centrally located in Angus Shire in the east of Scotland, bound by Dundee to the south, and the River Esk to the north. Of the approximate 308 Herald births in the period between 1555 and 1850, 85% of them within Angus shire. The parishes in Perthshire (mainly Meigle) and Fifeshire (Ferry Port on Craig) next to Angus recorded the next highest counts of births within the period.

The Herald name in Angus in 1555 was predominantly spelt as 'Herauld' in the Monifieth, Tannadice and Kettins parishes until around the last decade of the 1700s, where the 'u' was dropped from the name. No births with the Herauld spelling were recorded in Scotland after 1797 in Kirkden.

---

[1] as per births recorded by ScotlandPeople.co.uk, with the recorded surname of Herald, Herauld, and phonetic variances of the name.

Birth, Death and Marriages of the Herald name: Scotland 1555 – 1850

	Shire	Births	Deaths	Marriages
1	Angus	260	69	121
2	Perth	28	0	19
3	Fife	10	5	5
4	Kincardine	3	1	2
5	Aberdeen	2	2	2
6	Midlothian	2	3	2
7	Peebles	2	0	1
8	Ross	1	0	0
	Glasgow	0	0	1
	Argyll	0	0	1
	Lanark	0	0	1
		308	85	49

Gender Split: Scotland 1555 – 1850

The spilt between male (163) and female (143) births slightly favoured males. The most common names for each gender, including variants, were:

Male		Females	
James	34	Janet	33
John	31	Margaret	23
David	22	Elizabeth	21
William	22	Isabell	17
Alexander	12	Ann	15

Herald Births in Scotland by Shire
1555 - 1850

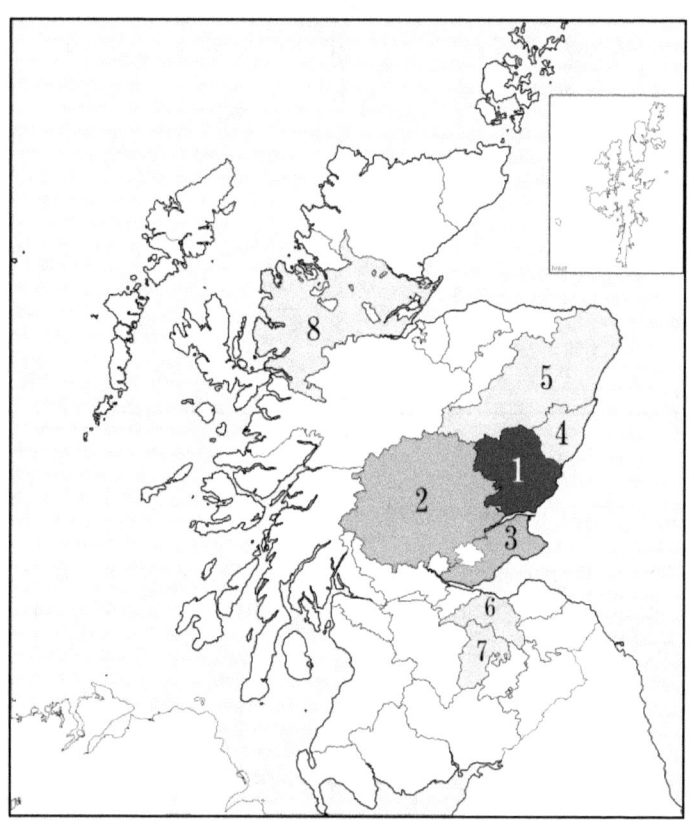

The Herald Family Name in Angus-shire

Within Angus shire, the Herald family were predominantly found in the parishes of Tannadice and Kirriemuir in the centre of the shire, and the coastal parish of Arbroath and St Vigeans. Tannadice recorded 42 births in the period, from 14 different couples, Kirriemuir recorded 29 births from 13 couples, and Arbroath and St Vigeans recorded 28 births from just 5 couples.

John was a predominant male name in Tannadice. James was a predominant male name in Kirriemuir, whereas the Arbroath and St Vigeans, Andrew and George appear as first names and neither name was present in the previous two.

Elizabeth, Anne, and Isabel were the predominant female name in Tannadice, whereas Kirriemuir went with Elspet and Jean. Again, Arbroath and St Vigeans had names not seen in the other parishes such as Louisa, Grizel, and Catherine.

Considering that Scottish families at the time tended to name their children in order of the patriarchal parents first, then the matriarchal parents before using other names, it can be theorised that the Tannadice/Kirriemuir Heralds and the Arbroath & St Vigeans Herald families were not directly related in the mid-1800s.

Herald Births in Angus-shire
1555 - 1850

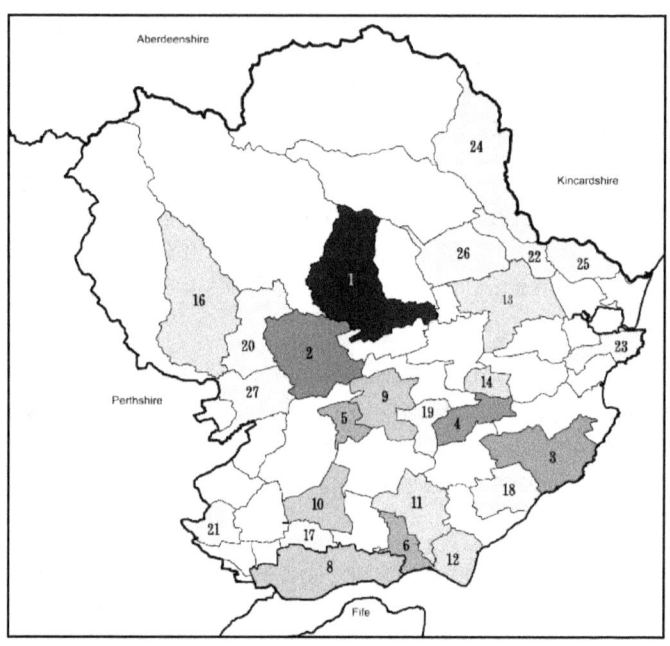

Births Count per Parish and Gender

	Angus Parish	Births	Male	Female
1	Tannadice	42	30	12
2	Kirriemuir	29	15	14
3	Arbroath and St Vigeans	28	10	18
4	Kirkden	16	8	8
5	Kinnettles	15	6	9
6	Monifieth	15	8	7
7	Kettins*	14	6	8
8	Dundee	14	9	5
9	Forfar	13[1]	6	6
10	Tealing	13[1]	6	6
11	Monikie	12	6	6
12	Barry	8	4	4
13	Brechin	7	6	1
14	Guthrie	6	3	3
15	Coupar Angus*	5	1	4
16	Lintrathen	5	2	3
17	Mains and Strathmartine	4	4	0
18	Arbirlot	2	0	2
19	Dunnichen	2	2	0
20	Kingoldrum	2	1	1
21	Lundie and Fowlis	2	2	0
22	Stracathro	1	1	0
23	Craig	1	1	0
24	Edzell	1	1	0
25	Logie Pert	1	1	0
26	Menmuir	1	1	0
27	Airlie	1	1	0
		260	141	117

* now a parish of Perthshire   1 = a birth did not have a gender recorded

Herald Given Names
Top 5 Parishes in Angus

Male

Tannadice	Kirriemuir	Arbroath & St Vigeans	Kirkden	Kinnettles
John	James	Andrew	Thomas	George
James	John	James	George	William
David	David	John	Andrew	Alexander
William	William	Thomas	George	
Alexander	Thomas	George	William	
George	Alexander	William		
Charles				
Robert				

Female

Tannadice	Kirriemuir	Arbroath & St Vigeans	Kirkden	Kinnettles
Anne	Elspet	Janet	Jean	Janet
Isobel	Isabel	Louisa	Margaret	Ann
Elisabeth	Jean	Ann	Mary	Margaret
Agnes	Helen	Margaret	Isobel	Elizabeth
Janet	Margaret	Agnes	Ann	Barbara
Barbara	Katherine	Elspet		
	Mary	Grizel		
	May	Catherine		
		Isabella		
		Mary		

ALEXANDER HERALD
FAMILY HISTORY

Alexander Herald Family Tree

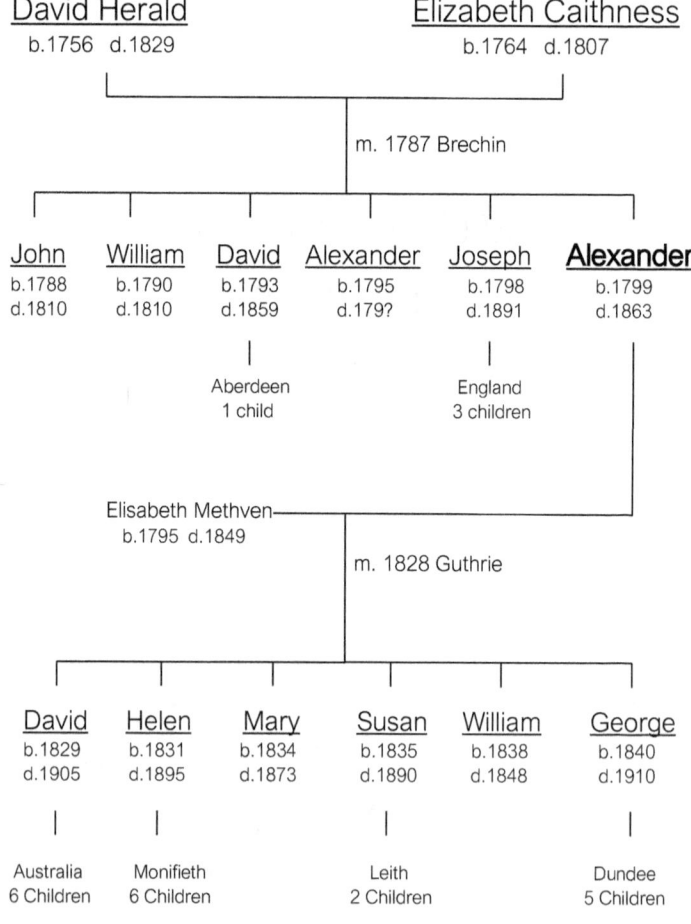

Stracathro 1764

Stracathro parish is small, mainly agricultural parish in Angus shire, Scotland; nearly 75% of the available land is used to cultivate crops. The agricultural revolution in that had commenced in the lowlands of Scotland had not yet reached Stracathro in 1764, farms were still run by tenant farmers, cottars, and yeomen, under the purview of the local landowner. In 1764, Stracathro was owned by Colin Mackenzie, having purchased it that year from Peter Turnbull.

Stracathro itself has a long history, with King Balliol submitting to King Edward I of England in the medieval church yard at Stracathro in 1296. It is only through his abdication that led Robert the Bruce to claiming the Scottish throne 10 years later. The current church at Stracathro was built in the 1800s at the same site.

The farming during the 17th century was mainly for crops that could be processed at nearby mills - namely corn, flax and meal. It would be several more years before the changes from the agricultural revolution would be felt in Stracathro. New improvements to farming techniques and newer crop types such as turnips, cabbages and potatoes were being introduced, as to, the farming of sheep. This would eventually see tenant farmers, cottars and yeomen removed from the properties as the landowners moved to cheaper methods of farming that required less people.

Elizabeth Caithness

Elizabeth Caithness was born at Ardo farm in Stracathro, on the 28th November 1764, the daughter of David

Caithness and Agnes Ordie. The Caithness family, and their various branches are a well-known family of the area, being involved in farming and the community.

Considering that the Caithness family had a presence at Ardo farm in 1795 when Elizabeth delivered her son Alexander, it is very likely that David Caithness was a tenant farmer, and not a farm hand or labourer, as tenant farmers tended to stay at locations for longer periods of time. At the time of Elizabeths marriage in 1787, her father had moved to Keithock farm in Brechin, where her brother John passed away in 1786.

Ardo farm is one of the larger farms in the area, and in 1792 it was a significantly large farm at 432 Scots acres [388 modern acres]2. There were several mills in the Stracathro area, to process local crops that would have been grown at Ardo, including corn, oats and wheat including the Pert Mill in Logie Pert, Brathinch Mill in Stracathro, and several mills in Brechin, including West Mill where David Herald worked at the end of the 1790s. Considering the size of Ardo farm, cattle may have been kept as stock for milk and/or beef.

As the daughter of a tenant farmer, Elizabeth would have assisted her mother in the domestic duties of the household. This may have entitled assisting in milking (if there were indeed milking cows), egg collection, cleaning and running the household. She would have attended church at Stracathro each Sunday morning, and travelled to town (Brechin) regularly with her parents.

---

[2] As noted on the Estate plan: Stracathro, the seat and property of Patrick Cruickshank, Esq. 1792

STRACATHRO ESTATE 1832

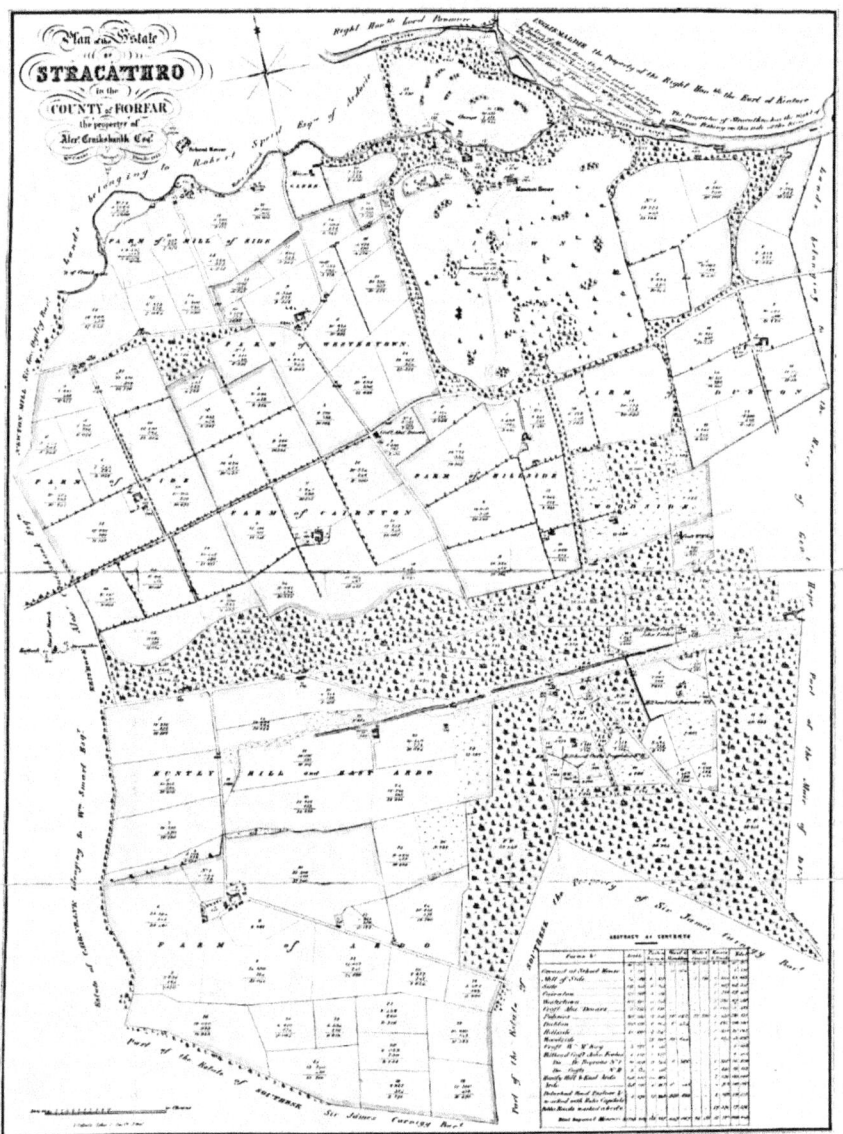

Reproduced with the permission of the National Library of Scotland

Brechin 1787

Brechin is one of the larger towns in the Angus area, lying closer to Dundee than Aberdeen to its north. It has a long and varied history, being the location of several battles against the English, and the location of one of only three 10th century round towers. Brechin Castle was used in a stand against King Edward I in 1303.

Brechin was in the midst of the industrial revolution at the turn of the 19th Century. Several new mills had opened, with new jobs in textile mills and bleaching fields becoming available. The shift away from agriculture into industry transformed the town, turning Brechin into a hub of the textiles industry in the north-east of Scotland.

'THE PROSPECT OF YE TOWN OF BRECHIN'

Reproduced with the permission of the National Library of Scotland

At the turn of the century, a famine had impacted crops across Scotland, which effected the local Brechin people with food shortages and poverty. Provisions became quite expensive; the town council was required to aid the increasing numbers of unfortunate. Travel was still by foot, with some wealthier people and businesses owning horses and carts. The Mail Coach was still 40 years away, with news from the south travelling slowly. Horses were expensive to own: there was a farm horse tax applied to horses in 1797-98 of 2 shillings and 3 pence per horse.

David Herald

The exact origins of David Herald have not been able to be confirmed with absolute certainty as a number of records that may have confirmed cannot be located (death certificate for either David or Elizabeth). Records show that David and Elizabeth were married in Brechin in 1787, when Elizabeth's father lived at Keithock farm in Brechin. The most likely candidate is David Herauld, born in 1756 to John Herauld and Isobel Vollum, at Miltonbank farm in Tannadice. This is mainly as David and Elizabeths eldest son is named John, and only one John Herald had a son called David within the key timeframe, within Angus shire.

At the time of his marriage in 1787, David Herald worked as a labourer to Provost Molinar in Brechin. The provost at the time was John Molinar (younger), who finished office in 1789, and passed away in 1791. The various birth records of his children shows that David changed jobs regularly in the period up to 1798, likely as David did not have any trade or education that would have resulted in a higher positioned job. All the employment that David had was manual, lowly paid positions. At the birth of his first son John in 1788,

MAP OF BRECHIN 1794

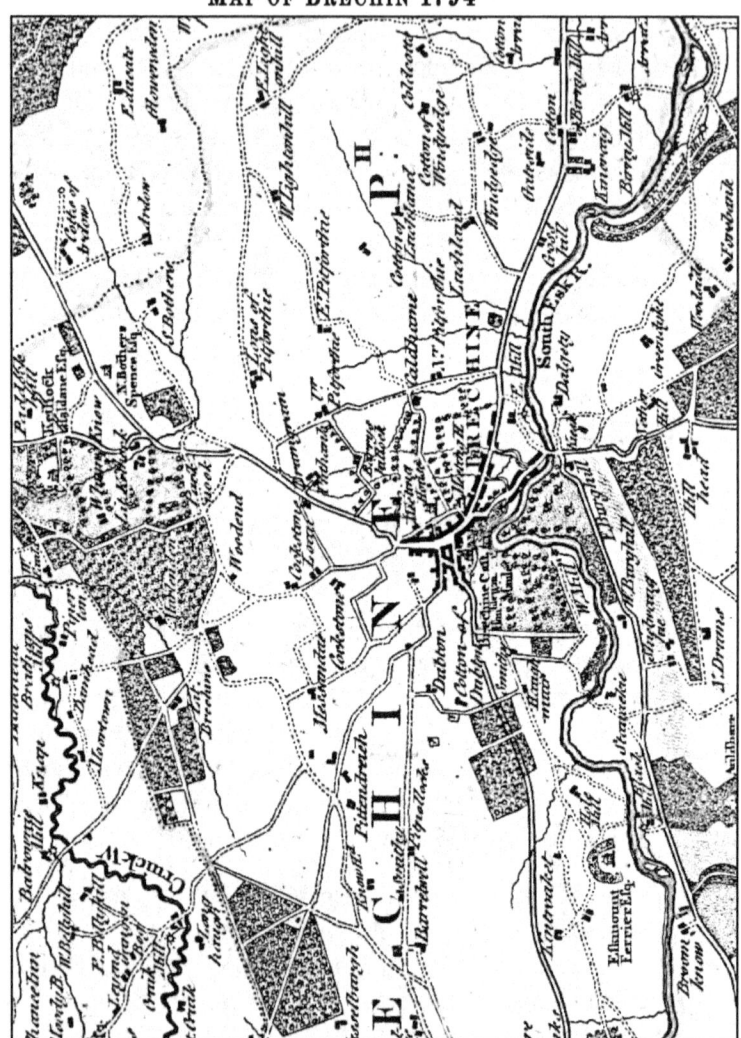

Showing: West Mill, and Ardo, Keithock and Hillhead farms
Reproduced with the permission of the National Library of Scotland

David is noted as a subtenant at Hillhead farm to the south of the city. The birth record of his next son William, David is a servant to Bailie John Smith. He was again a labourer at Hillhead farm in 1792 when his third son David was born, then as a labourer at West Mill, a local mill at Brechin from 1798 onwards (births of sons Joseph and Alexander).

West Mill was a water-powered meal mill, owned by the Boyack family, which commenced operations in 1695. West Mill appears to have failed sometime after 1800, as it is noted on the 1794 map of Brechin, there is no trace of it on the maps produced from 1840 onwards. West Mill was situated on the west side of the River Esk, just south of Brechin Castle and the castle grounds.

Life as a labourer in a mill at the turn of the 19th century was manually intensive and physically dangerous. Wages were typically low, hours long, and injuries were commonplace. As labourer at a meal mill, David Heralds' duties would typically have included feeding the grain into the mill, collecting, and bagging the flour, sifting, and storing it into finer flours types, maintenance duties ensuring that the mill is kept operational, and delivery of the product to the towns. Days would have typically been between 12 and 14 hours in length, and pay around £12 per annum. David was fortunate have employment, even if it paid poorly.

In an article published in the Arbroath Guide on October 19, 1867, the writer reminiscences on his time as a Brechin Youth Volunteer (commenced in 1803) and a trip they took to Arbroath to practice their drilling skills. The writer fondly recalls the trip with Colonel Molison family including Tom Molison, and recounts how they were joined by "David Herald, with the West Mill cart." Taking into account the various people in the writing, it is likely this trip took place around 1805.

In 1807, David Heralds' wife Elizabeth passed, and three years later his two oldest sons, John (aged 22) and William (aged 20) died from disease. While records do not show what this may have been, there had been outbreaks of small pox, scarlet fever and measles throughout Scotland and the British Isles during the early part of the century, which mainly affected those of the working class and poor.

The records show that the Heralds moved from Brechin after Elizabeths death. The Guthrie Kirk records for the period between 1808 and 1828 detail David Herald as an officer of the church, who was paid a wage of £4 annually. This position would have included the maintenance of the parish church, and possibly keeping the church accounts: basically relating to the income of the parish church and the expenditure on the maintenance of the parish church. The records state David resigned on June 22, 1828 which fit into the assumed year of death 1829 (as per Alexanders poetry). The Guthrie kirk burial records unfortunately appear to have been lost to the passing of time.

MY FIRST VISIT TO ARBROATH.

Volunteering was the rage in my early years as it is now again the fashion: I say rage advisedly, for the spirit of soldiering pervaded all ages, and was equally strong in the Man, the Lad, and the Boy. At the school there were then, as may yet occasionally be seen, the little men with paper caps, lath swords, a penny trumpet, and an old kettle for a drum, parading with great majesty, the captain having paper epaulettes to distinguish him from the common men. How it may be now I cannot tell, but in my time the places of honour, the posts most desired, were those of Captain and Drummer, and great was the contest to obtain the epaulettes or the tin kettle. Of these corps we had then in Brechin as many as a dozen or more. Marching about, beating our drum, and displaying our handkerchiefs for flags was our chief exercise. But there was a more pretentious company—the Brechin Juvenile Volunteers, commanded by Captain Laing, whose Head Quarters were at the Meikle Mill, the youngest lad in which Corps was fourteen at least, and who, having contrived to obtain a flag, a drum, and a fife, with a real sword for the Captain, were obliged to content themselves with wooden guns for the single soldiers, but who were regularly drilled to the then complicated manual exercise. All these lads, as they grew up, entered the local militia, and most of them I believe joined the regular army. Captain Laing himself enlisted in the marines, from which corps he was discharged at the peace, holding the office of sergeant, and although he afterwards became a schoolmaster he was through life known as Sergeant Laing. However, the local militia, originally volunteers, but put under martial law by that name,—the local militia of four companies was the grand corps, and connected with them was my first visit to Arbroath, my first acquaintance with the residents under the patronage of Saint

Thomas. The militia assembled weekly for drill in companies on the Inch of Brechin. They were then in their every-day clothes, clean and neat, but not in uniform, and after so many hours' drill, the companies were dismissed, each man receiving a shilling for his attendance. Once a month or so the companies assembled as a regiment in full regimentals on the West Mill Parks, and went through more complicated manœuvres under charge of Colonel Molison and of Major Ogilvy, mounted, as a major should be, on horseback. Of course there was the local poet who recorded in verse the doings of these great heroes; but I now only remember two lines of the poem, or song, or whatever it was; and these two lines, I daresay, are sufficient:

<blockquote>
Brave Major Ogilvie, he sits upon his horse,
He makes them all obey, he speaks with such a voce.
</blockquote>

Drilling at Brechin was all very well; but Government wanted to give the local militia some ideas of military life from home; and hence it was that our Brechin Volunteers were sent, not into camps or cantonments, but into comfortable quarters for six weeks each year at Arbroath, for what was called permanent duty. Duty, did I say? It was play, and the greatest play imaginable; and many a grand ploy arose out of the permanent duty. Father was at Arbroath on permanent duty, billeted on a family that would rather want him, and who gave him a small sum to be quit of him. Mother and bairns had no pirns to fill, as father was from home, and they wanted sea-bathing. Father hired a room, and all hied to Arbroath to enjoy themselves, leaving the loom in Brechin standing idle. A soldier's life for six weeks in summer, in a bonny burrows town, with wife and bairns alongside; a change of scene, a change of food, a change of air—was it not a grand ploy? But the ploy was not confined to the common soldier, his wife and bairns: the relatives of the officers had their share of the amusement; and hence it was that I, *faitherless bairn*, got a trip to Arbroath along with Colonel Molison's family, because I had an uncle who held a Captain's commission.

Such a trip was really a ploy to lads like Tom Molison and me. We had heard a great deal about the 'Round O' of the Abbey of Arbroath, and believed that in reality the whole letters of the alphabet had once stood in stone and lime, but that John Knox had caused all to be destroyed except this one letter, that the people might cry Oh! against the abominations of the Roman Catholics. Well, one summer morning we were all assembled at Provost Molison's gate—for Mr Molison was then permanent Provost, as well as permanent Colonel—and David Herald having come in with the West Mill cart, off we set; not like Duncan Macallaghin, a gallopin', gallopin', but at a decent walking pace, such as a cart-horse of those days might be expected to take. We reached Arbroath about eleven o'clock, having stopped midway to feed man and horse—the passengers fed all the way. The Abbey and 'Round O' attracted our attention at a distance, but excited little of our curiosity when we entered Arbroath, our soldiers occupying our minds wholly. When we arrived at the White Hart Inn, then kept by the Misses Fielden, we found a guard parading in front of the door of the Inn, which was an old fashioned house off the street, with an outside stair. Some soldiers in undress came to aid David Herald, and we youngsters were taken into the bar and kindly treated by the worthy ladies. And was it not grand, when I went out with my uncle, to have the guard present arms to me? By-and-bye the trumpet sounded, the soldiers assembled in companies and marched to the Common for exercise. All this we had seen in Brechin, but the sea, the Shore, and the ships, were things new to us, and excited our admiration; and I think we were more astonished to find the High Street terminate in the ocean than we were with anything else. The Abbey somehow disappointed us. There, to be sure, was the muckle O, but where were the A.B.C.? Nothing but heaps of rubbish (all now cleared away) lay around. But the important point was the dinner. Tom Molison and I were asked to mess with the officers; the band played the 'Roast Beef of Old England;' the officers assembled in an anteroom; the fugler gave notice dinner was on the table; the officers marched into the dining-room according to their rank; the Colonel and Major took wine with each other, and then with every officer in succession, and we little ones were not forgotten. After dinner 'The King' was drunk in style; the 'Army and Navy followed;' and then we boys were sent to Misses Fielden to get tea in the bar, and a capital tea we did get from the kind old ladies, who sent us away about seven o'clock in the evening, loaded with partans and buckies. Cruisin, a blind beggar who travelled the country in those days, dined not with the officers, but after them, sitting on the steps of the large outside stair, and comfortably he did dine, supplied with everything by one of the Misses Fielden, whose charity we believe was unbounded, and who kept themselves poor by their liberality. In their latter years they were aided by an annuity purchased for them by the gentlemen of the town and neighbourhood. Cruisin is gone, the Misses Fielden are gone, the officers and most of the men are all gone: we are only aware of the existence of one soldier of the regiment: David Herald and all my fellow-travellers are gone, and I only remain to tell a tale, perhaps not worth the telling. It was a long day, as it was eleven o'clock at night till we reached Brechin, but, like all other long days, it had an end, as has this story. Tom Molison and I slept most of the way home, and likely my reader is ready to sleep as he reads this. C. S.

Arbroath Times, Digital Image © British Library

Guthrie 1826

Guthrie is a small parish, centrally located between Brechin, Forfar and Arbroath in Angus-shire, with two portions – the northern had being centred around Guthrie Castle, and the southern border around the hamlet of Kirkbuddo. The population of Guthrie in the mid-1800s was around 500, mainly employed in agriculture. Guthrie only contained one mill, and no manufacturers of any type, limiting employment opportunities. The largest hamlet in the parish was the Kirktown situated directly to the east of Guthrie Castle, with a small cluster of houses and the parish church.

Forfar is the closest of the larger towns, being 7 miles distance, however the chief mode of communications came from Arbroath on the coast, 8 miles distance.

Guthrie Castle was the chief residence of Laird Guthrie – at the time of Alexanders marriage and the publication of his book, this would have been John Guthrie, 17th Laird of Guthrie, who died in November 1845. This book was dedicated to John Guthrie, as his tenant, and his supporter.

Alexander Herald

Alexander Herald was born in Brechin on the 29th December 1799, the youngest son of David and Elizabeth. One of his older brothers born in 1795 at Ardo farm in Stracathro was also named Alexander, who would have died sometime between 1795 and 1799.

Alexanders mother died when he was 8 years old, and his two oldest brothers when he was 10. It is clear that

Alexander received some form of education, with the ability to both read and write. There was a local school at Brechin where he was born, which he would have likely attended.

The Herald family moved to Guthrie after Elizabeths death in 1807 as David Herald is recorded in the Guthrie parish records in 1808. Alexanders oldest remaining brother David was married in Guthrie in 1818, and Alexander himself married Elisabeth Methven in 1826 at Guthrie Church. Alexander would remain in Guthrie for the remainder of his life. His other brother Joseph left Scotland altogether and married in London, England in 1823.

Alexander is recorded as both the grocer and the post master of Guthrie in the 1841 and 1851 Scottish census. The postal services in Scotland lagged significantly behind England in the mid-1700s, due to distances as well as a very limited number of towns included within the postal routes. This changed significantly in the first quarters of the 1800s, with the number of postal towns doubling, and the frequency of postal services increasing. The Scotland wide penny post – post offices that also included the additional charges for the delivery of newspapers, saw the rapid expansion. The Scotland National Penny Post was implemented in 1840.

As Post Master in Guthrie, Alexander was responsible for the sorting and delivery of post to the local Guthrie area. The post would have been firstly routed to the nearest larger postal town – Arbroath - before being taken to Guthrie. It is possible that Alexander may have gone into Arbroath himself to pick up the local mail.

Post Masters worked very long hours for what was not considered fair pay, taking into account the considerable time and effort they undertook, as well as being required to frank each post and charge accordingly.

Alexander and his wife had 6 children – David, Helen, Mary, Susan, William and George. Their daughters all left home as teenagers to work as servants in Arbroath, with Susan returning home with an illegitimate child when she was 24. Their oldest son David moved to Aberdeen to work as a rail clerk.

Both Alexander and his wife both suffered from ailments that limited their lives. During this time, Alexander wrote poetry. His poem 'The Maid of the Valley' was published in one of the local papers during this period.

Elisabeth Methven died in 1849, after a long illness. Their unmarried daughter, Mary, returned home to perform domestic duties for their father until his death in 1863. She died unmarried in Monifieth in 1873. Alexander and Elisabeth were buried at Guthrie church, although there are no headstones marking their graves.

OLD GUTHRIE POST OFFICE, GUTHRIE

(NOW A PRIVATE RESIDENCE)

Articles in Local Papers regarding Amusements of Solitude

Montrose Review: November 14 1845

> Just published, price 3s.,
> Dedicated by permission to JOHN GUTHRIE, Esq. of Guthrie,
> A VOLUME of POETRY, entitled 'AMUSEMENTS of SOLITUDE.' By ALEXANDER HERALD, Merchant, Guthrie.
> Arbroath: Published by STEWART GELLATLY; sold also by JAMES LUNDIE. Montrose: ALEX. ROGERS. Dundee: WM. MIDDLETON. Edinburgh: JOHN MENZIES. 1845.

Arbroath Guide: November 15 1845

> HERALD'S POEMS.—To a little volume of Poems, entitled "Amusement's of Solitude," by Mr Alexander Herald, Guthrie, lately issued from the Arbroath press, we beg to call the particular attention of the public. Many of the pieces are written with great taste and feeling, giving evidence of the author being deeply imbued with a love of poetry, and of not having courted the muse in vain. A sweet simplicity, and an easy flowing versification, are the chief attractions of the little volume; and when we have to add that most of the pieces were composed by their amiable author while suffering from infirmity, brought on by many years of ill health, and that the composition of them served as a solace to him under the trying circumstances in which he was placed, often serving as a balm to the wounded spirit, we feel certain that they will be read with peculiar interest, and their appearance meet with that support to which so many circumstances justly entitle them. We may add that the little volume is got up in a particularly neat form, and that its price places it within the reach of all who desire to patronise real merit.

Alexanders Children

David Herald

David moved to Aberdeen when he was 15, where he worked as a rail clerk and eventually an accountant. He married Margaret Beatrice Houston in Aberdeen in 1853, and emigrated to Melbourne, Australia soon after. He worked as an accountant, until his retirement, and died in 1905 in Melbourne. He had 6 children: Alexander, David Houston, John William, George, Jane Elizabeth and Mary Wilhemina.

John passed as a baby, and George in his early 20s. Jane and Mary remained unmarried and childless. Alexander moved to Queensland in his early 20s and moved around significantly, being married in Balranald NSW, having a daughter in Broken Hill NSW, who died at 6 months and buried in Wilcannia NSW, before having a son in Tasmania who pass soon after. Alexander died in Cloncurry QLD.

Only David Houston had children that survived to adult hood. David Houston married Christina Lowe Russell (her family came from Pittenweem, Fife) and became a successful solicitor in Melbourne, along with his oldest son David Russell Herald. David Russell had one child – a son.

At one stage, David Houston and his family lived at Labassa Mansion, a now heritage listed property in Caulfield East, an affluent suburb of Melbourne. His middle son died at 22, and his youngest son, to his second wife Ethel, was an RAAF pilot in World War II. His short marriage did not produce any children.

Helen Methven Herald

Helen Methven Herald married Alexander Reid in 1858, and had 6 children: James, Mary, Alexander, Susan, John, and Helen Elizabeth. She died in Monifieth, Angus-shire in 1895. One of Helens' grandsons was Prof. Graeme Cochrane Moodie, the founder of the School of Politics at the University of York.

Mary Herald

Mary Herald remained unmarried, and died in 1873. She worked as a servant in St Vigeans in 1851, before returning to Guthrie to look after her father after her mothers' passing.

Susan Herald

Susan Herald was 12 years old when her mother passed in 1849. By 1851, she was working as a servant in a residence in Arbroath on the Angus shire coast. Susan gave birth to an illegitimate daughter in 1861 and returned to live with her father in Guthrie. She eventually married James McAuley in 1878, had one son in 1880, and died in Leith in 1890.

William Herald

William was born in 1838, he is recorded in the 1841 census at Guthrie, aged 3. No death record can be located, however, the copy of Alexanders book held by the National

Library in Scotland has handwritten notes by Alexander that note William died of scarlet fever in January 1848.

George Herald

George Herald married Lucy McHardy in 1870 and moved to Dundee. They had 5 children: Maria, William, Alexander, Georgina and David. George was employed as a gardener, and worked at Kinniard House in Perthshire in 1901. When he died in 1910, his estate was worth £777 – good savings for a gardener of the era.

His daughter Maria remained unmarried. The census in 1901 lists her as a servant in Blair Athol, where she was buried in 1945. Georgina married John Stratton and had one daughter.

George's oldest son William became a butcher in Dundee, married Isabella and had 3 children. Alexander made a career in joinery/cabinet making in Dundee, but does not appear to have had children. David – the youngest son – died as a baby.

Alexanders Brothers

John Herald

Died at the age of 22.

William Herald

Died at the age of 20.

David Herald

David married Margaret Young in Guthrie in 1818. They moved to Aberdeen at some time before 1841, where he is recorded as a cow-keeper in the census. A 13-year-old female is also on the census record – Emma Herald, born in 1828 in Ireland, but no birth or death record can be located. Emma is not recorded on the 1851 census. No other children appear to have been born to the couple. David died in Aberdeen in 1859.

Alexander Herald

Alexander Herald (1795) died sometime between 1975 and 1799 before Alexander (b. 1799) was born.

Joseph Herald

Joseph Herald moved to London, England, and married Harriet Ashford in 1823. Joseph is noted as a gentleman's servant in the 1861 census, just before his death in August of the same year. He had 3 children: Emma, Edmund Richard and Alfred Joseph.

Emma married John Price, a tailor, and worked as a dressmaker in Marylebone, London. They had one daughter who remained unmarried and did not have any children.

Josephs sons both emigrated to Sydney, Australia in the mid-1850s, with Edmund Richard becoming the first Station Master at the new Liverpool railway and the first employee of the newly formed Sydney Railways with any experience in trains. There was a significant write up in the Sydney papers on his contribution to Australia on his death in 1922. Edmund had 11 children with his second wife Adeline.

One of Edmunds children Adeline Rebecca Herald married Victor Claude Saywell, who was brutally murdered in his bed and Adeline beaten almost to death in one of Australia's biggest unsolved murder mysteries. Their eldest son Jack was the key suspect, and he went on to become a well-known racing car driver.

Alfred Joseph Herald was a real estate agent who had 10 children with his wife Maria Murphy (from Ireland). His children added 21 grandchildren, who all remained in Australia. His grandson William Sharpe Hannah Herald won a silver medal in swimming at the 1920 Olympics in Antwerp, Belgium.

With Thanks

Information for the history section of this book was made possible from the assistance and knowledge of the following organisations and people:

Angus Archives
Restenneth Priory
Forfar, Scotland
www.angusalive.scot

National Library of Scotland
Edinburgh, Scotland
www.nls.uk

Scotland's People
www.scotlandspeople.gov.uk

Stracathro Estates
Hugh Campbell Adamson – Director
www.stracathro.com

References

Black, D; *The History of Brechin to 1864*; 1867; Edinburgh.

Gauldie, E; *Scottish Country Miller 1700-1900: History of water-powered meal milling in Scotland*; 1981; Edinburgh

Harris, B.; *The Post Office and the Making of North Britain, c. 1750–c. 1840;* Journal of Scottish Historical Studies, Volume 43 Issue 1, Page 1-30.

Smount, T.C, and Fenton, A; *Scottish Agriculture before the Improvers - an Exploration*; British Agricultural History Society

W. Blackwood and Sons; *The New Statistical Account of Scotland: Forfar, Kincardine*; 1845

Images

Ainslie, John; *Map of the county of Forfar or Shire of Angus*; 1794

Estate plan: *Stracathro, the seat and property of Patrick Cruickshank Esq.*; 1792

Montrose Review; *Amusements of Solitude Advertisement*; November 14, 1845

Morris, Lydon, and Fawcett; *Brechin Castle - A Series of Picturesque Views of Seats of Noblemen and Gentlemen of Great Britain and Ireland*; 1880.

Slezer, John; *'The Prospect of ye Town of Brechin'*; 1693

The Arbroath Guide; *My First Visit to Arbroath*; Saturday, October 19, 1867

The Arbroath Guide; *Heralds Poems Review*; November 15, 1845

JL Herald is an Australian author of two poetry books: toxic/empathy and before/after. She is known for exploring difficult topics in a raw and open manner.

http://www.jlherald-poet.com

www.ingramcontent.com/pod-product-compliance
Lightning Source LLC
Chambersburg PA
CBHW072005290426
44109CB00018B/2143